DIRT

Terence McLaughlin

ECHO POINT BOOKS & MEDIA, LLC
Brattleboro, Vermont

Published by Echo Point Books & Media
Brattleboro, Vermont
www.EchoPointBooks.com

Copyright © 1971, 2020 Terence McLaughlin

Dirt
ISBN: 978-1-62654-945-4 (casebound)
          978-1-62654-946-1 (paperback)

Cover design by Kaitlyn Whitaker

Cover image: London's water supply, 1828 caricature by
George Cruikshank; courtesy of Science Photo Library
*Historical artwork by the British caricaturist George
Cruikshank (1792-1878), showing people protesting
against sewage polluting London's water supply. At centre,
John Edwards, the owner of the Southwark Water Works
is sitting on a toilet with a chamberpot on his head, on a
globe in the Thames, raising a goblet of polluted water to
the crowds on the river bank. Dead animals are on the
trident in his hand. Sewers bring excrement into the river,
and washer women (left) attempt to clean clothes. In the
background is London Bridge and the sailing ships and
buildings of early 19th century London. Unlike the owners
of other water companies, Edwards had failed to improve
the sourcing and quality of the drinking water he supplied,
despite an 1828 report calling for reforms.*

To Eve
Who first made history interesting

Contents

1	Introduction	1
2	A Scene of Pomp and Luxury	7
3	The Dance of Death	15
4	An Ounce of Civet	34
5	Over the Nasty Sty	47
6	Sweete Themmes Run Softly	59
7	That Unspeakable Puddle of a Time	69
8	Multitudes of Poor Pestiferous Creatures	80
9	The Yahoos	96
10	Like a Diamond Begrimed with Dirt	119
11	Oh God! What I Saw!	130
12	Fouling our own Nest	156
	Select Bibliography	169
	Index	173

Acknowledgements

Thanks are due to Messrs Routledge & Kegan Paul for permission to print two passages from *The Book of the Thousand Nights and One Night* (Fr. trans. Dr J. C. Mardrus; Eng. trans. E. Powys Mathers) 2nd ed. 1964, and to Edward Lucie-Smith and Penguin Books Ltd for permission to print lines from the modernized text of the *Egloges of Alexander Barclay* in *The Penguin Book of Satirical Verse*, ed. Lucie-Smith, 1967.

1. Introduction

Dirt is evidence of the imperfections of life, a constant reminder of change and decay. It is the dark side of all human activities—human, because it is only in our judgements that things are dirty: there is no such material as *absolute* dirt. Earth, in the garden, is a valuable support and nourishment for plants, and gardeners often run it through their fingers lovingly; earth on the carpet is dirt. A pile of dung, to the dung-beetle, is food and shelter for a large family; a pile of dung, to the Public Health Inspector, is a Nuisance. Soup in a plate, before we eat it, is food; the traces that we leave on the plate imperceptibly become dirt. Lipstick on a girl's lips may make her boy-friend more anxious to touch them with his own lips; lipstick on a cup will probably make him refuse to touch it.

Because of this relativity, because dirt can be almost anything that we choose to call dirt, it has often been defined as 'matter out of place'. This fits the 'earth (garden)/earth (carpet)' difference quite well, but it is not really very useful as a definition. A sock on the grand piano or a book in a pile of plates may be untidy, and they are certainly out of place, but they are not necessarily dirty. To be dirt, the material also has to be hard to remove and unpleasant. If you sit on the beach, particularly if you bathe, sand will stick to you, but not many people would classify this as *dirt*, mainly because it brushes off so easily. However, if, as often happens, the sand is covered with oil, tar, or sewage, and this sticks to you, it is definitely dirt.

Sartre, in his major philosophical work on Existentialism,

L'Être et le Néant, presents a long discussion on the nature of *sliminess* or stickiness which has quite a lot to do with our ideas of dirt. He points out that quite small children, who presumably have not yet learned any notions of cleanliness, and cannot yet be worried by germs, still tend to recognize that slimy things are unpleasant. It is because slimy things are clinging that we dislike them—they hold on to us even when we should like to let them go, and, like an unpleasant travelling companion or an obscene telephone caller, seem to be trying to involve us in themselves.

'If an object which I hold in my hands is solid,' says Sartre, 'I can let go when I please. . . . Yet here is the slimy reversing the terms . . . I open my hands, I want to let go of the slimy material and it sticks to me, it draws me, it sucks at me. Its mode of being is neither the reassuring inertia of the solid nor a dynamism like that in water which is exhausted in fleeing from me. It is a soft yielding action, a moist and feminine sucking, it *lives* obscurely under my fingers. . . .'

This is the feeling of *pollution*, the kind of experience where something dirty has attached itself to us and we cannot get rid of the traces, however hard we try. Ritual defilement is one aspect of this feeling, and one which provides an enormous field of study for anthropologists (when they are not engaged in their favourite activity of reviling one another), but powerful irrational feelings of defilement exist in the most sophisticated societies. Try serving soup in a chamber-pot. However clean it may be, and however much a certain type of guest may find it 'amusing', there will be a very real uneasiness about the juxtaposition. There are some kinds of dirt that we treat, in practice, as irremovable—as in the case of the old lady who was unlucky enough to drop her false teeth down the lavatory, where they were flushed into the sewer. When a search failed to find them, she heaved a sigh of relief. 'I would never have fancied them again,' she said, and most people would agree. Even things which in themselves are clean, but can be associated with dirt, tend to be suspect. Vance Packard, in *The Hidden Persuaders*, quotes the sad story of a company who tried to boost their sales of soup mix by offering free nylon stockings. The scheme was a complete fiasco. '. . . people seeing the offer were offended. Subconsciously they associated feet and soup and were alienated because they didn't like the idea of feet being in their soup.' Faced by such reactions from industrialized society, we are in a better position to understand such primitive taboos as the fact that, for instance, a women of the Lele tribe who is menstruating must not cook for her husband or even poke the fire that is used for cooking.

Sartre, in his analysis, goes on to discuss the fear and disgust inspired by slimy things. When we touch them, they not only cling to us, but the boundary line between ourselves and the slime is blurred—if we dip our fingers in oil or honey (Sartre's favourite exemplar—it is difficult to tell whether he likes honey or dislikes it so intensely as to have a fixation about it) it hangs in strings from our fingers, our hands seem to be dissolving in it:

'To touch slime is to risk being dissolved in sliminess. Now this dissolution by itself is frightening enough . . . but it is still more frightening in that the metamorphosis is not just into a *thing* (bad as that would be) but into slime. . . .'

There is a feeling of helplessness when you are faced by something slimy: the real horror to some of eating oysters is that, once the *thing* is in your mouth, there is no way of avoiding eating all of it. Other food of a strange character may be sampled in nibbles or sips, and if it is too distasteful you can stop; oysters take over the situation as the dominant partner. The same applies to the raw herrings beloved by the Dutch.

Unfortunately for our peace of mind, most of the products of the human body are slimy—saliva, mucus, excrement, pus, semen, blood, lymph—and even honest sweat gets sticky by evaporation. 'If I can fervently drink his tears,' wrote Genet, 'Why not so the limpid drop on the end of his nose?' And the answer is quite clear. The drop on the end of his nose is slimy. We do not wish to be associated so closely and so permanently with other human beings. Their various slimy secretions will pollute us, will bring us into a closer and more permanent relationship with them than we should wish.

Of course, our own secretions are different. We have learned to live with them. We do not object to our own saliva, for instance, but the idea of someone else's saliva touching us is usually repellent, just as we do not like to think of cooks tasting the food which we are going to eat. Brahmins carry this even further, and do not like their own saliva to touch their skin: if

3

a Brahmin accidentally touches his fingers to his lips he must bath or at least change his clothes, and this means that he has to eat by effectively throwing the food into his mouth. Spitting on other people is a sign of great loathing, and being spat on is extremely humiliating and disgusting, despite the fact that the saliva is mostly water. There was an old music-hall joke about a man called away from a public-house bar, leaving a full glass on the counter; to protect his drink he put up a little notice saying, 'I have spat in this beer.' When he returned the drink was still there, but there was an addition to the notice: 'So have I.'

We are tolerant of our own bodily functions and smells, like Mr. Bloom in *Ulysses* reading *Titbits* in the outside privy—'He read on, seated calm above his own rising smell'—and the Icelanders have a coarse but accurate proverb, that every man likes the smell of his own farts, but too much evidence of other people's bodily function is 'dirty'. We can extend some tolerance to the people we love, because the sense of close contact and lasting association is not then a matter of pollution. Lovers can share a cup or a bath with one another, and not worry about the close contact that this implies, but we do not extend this tolerance to the rest of humanity. Indeed, the whole act of sexual intercourse, without the tolerance induced by love and respect, would be hopelessly polluting and grotesque. Those who find it difficult to reconcile themselves to human contact often consider love-making a disgusting affair, like the lady who wrote to the *Bristol Evening Post* some years ago:

> Sex used to be treated with decent reticence—now it is discussed openly. This sort of thing can do immense harm. The moral standards accepted as 'normal' by most young people today are a case in point.
>
> Why our all-wise Creator should have chosen such a distasteful—even disgusting—means of reproducing humanity is a thing that I, personally, have never been able to understand.

Where the tolerance stops is a matter of taste. Those couples whose desire to 'merge' into one another is greater than their innate or acquired fear of pollution may resort to practices that appear 'dirty' to other people. Krafft-Ebing, in the *Psychopathia*

Sexualis, deals with the curious deviation of *coprolegny*, where people derive sexual pleasure from licking or touching the bodily secretions of others, including excrement. Bizarre as this habit may seem, the pages that follow will demonstrate that dirt is an entirely relative concept, and that there is no limit to the strangeness of people's attitudes to it. Coprophilia, the love of filth, can take all forms, from Aubrey Beardsley's joking references to it in *Under the Hill* and *Venus and Tannhäuser*, wher it seems to be introduced out of a scholarly wish to include *everything*, to a complete acceptance and even enjoyment of living conditions and bodily habits that seem disgusting.

On this crowded planet, it is very difficult to get away from contact with other people, and the traces they leave behind them. In the countryside, if we settle down to rest or picnic, we do not consider pine cones, dead sticks, leaves, pebbles, earth, or anything else *natural* strewn over the ground as dirt, or even as litter, and we are not likely to be very worried even by rabbit droppings and other traces of animal life, but paper bags, beer cans, and other signs of human life make us annoyed, and human excrement left in the open will probably make us look for another place to sit. It is the human traces that we object to, because we fear contamination, a kind of magical power that these traces might exert on us if we happened to touch them or even smell them. We dislike the feeling that these unknown people who have been in the place before us may somehow infect us with their own diseases and shortcomings, and their lives may be permanently entwined with ours, just as the Thieves in Circle VIII of the *Inferno* lose their individual likenesses and are constantly melting one into another. This is not just a fear of germs, for the feelings date from pre-Pasteur days, and are shared, or even intensified, in primitive societies where no notions of the germ theory exist. 'And this shall be his uncleanness in his issue: whether his flesh run with his issue, or his flesh be stopped from his issue, it is his uncleanness. Every bed, whereon he lieth that hath the issue, is unclean: and every thing, whereon he sitteth, shall be unclean. And whosoever toucheth his bed shall wash his clothes, and bathe himself in water, and be unclean until the even. And he that sitteth on any thing whereon he sat that hath the issue shall wash his clothes, and bathe himself in water, and be unclean until the even. . . .' And so on, in *Leviticus* chapters xi to xv, in passages that the well-known Biblical interpreter Nathaniel Micklem has called 'the least attractive in the whole Bible. To the modern reader there is much in them that is meaningless or repulsive.' Of course we know now that such regulations helped to prevent the spread of infectious diseases, and that the orthodox Jews who followed these hygienic laws managed to survive plague periods and other epidemics better than the mass of the population, but the founders of the law were working only on instinct and the formalization of instinct that we call ritual. The Jewish hygienic rules may be stricter than many other systems, but they are not different in kind. An orthodox Jew's abstention from pork is no more logical or illogical than his Christian neighbour's abstention from dog or cat; both feelings are deeply held, and have nothing to do with the habits of the animals themselves. Those writers who try to explain away such customs as the results of semi-scientific investigation often say that Jews abstain from pork because the pig is dirty, or because pork is more liable to *Salmonella* infection than other meat. Both statements are true, but if these were the only reasons, Jews and Christians should be eating cats, who have very clean habits, or guinea-pigs, who keep themselves free from vermin. The purely hygienic laws, about leprosy, skin diseases, menstruation, and discharges from the body, are not based on bacteriology, they are based on avoidance of defilement by other people.

We are all jealous of our 'one-ness', our individuality, and we resent and fear any situation that forces us to become intimate, in the real sense of the word, with another person against our will. Contamination by other people is what we really fear about dirt: Sartre says, in *Huis Clos*, that Hell is other people. Dirt is also other people.

2. *A Scene of Pomp and Luxury*

'The stupendous aqueducts,' wrote Gibbon, 'so justly celebrated by the praises of Augustus himself, replenished the *Thermae*, or baths, which had been constructed in every part of the city, with Imperial magnificence. The baths of Antoninus Caracalla, which were open, at stated hours, for the indiscriminate service of the senators and the people, contained above sixteen hundred seats of marble; and more than three thousand were reckoned in the baths of Diocletian. The walls of the lofty apartments were covered with curious mosaics, that imitated the art of the pencil in the elegance of design and the variety of colours. The Egyptian granite was beautifully encrusted with the precious green marble of Numidia; the perpetual stream of hot water was poured into the capacious basins through so many wide mouths of bright and massy silver; and the meanest Roman could purchase, with a small copper coin, the daily enjoyment of a scene of pomp and luxury which might excite the envy of kings of Asia.'*

The actual size of the 'lofty apartments' is difficult to grasp: the baths of Caracalla covered a site, roughly square, and about 1100 feet each way, or a total covered space of nearly 28 acres, six times the total site area of St. Paul's Cathedral. The baths, and the general water supply, came from aqueducts carrying water to Rome from the surrounding countryside: the longest overhead portion, built on arches, was about fourteen miles in length, but by A.D. 52 there was a total of 220 miles of

* *Decline and Fall of the Roman Empire*, chapter 31.

channelling carrying, at peak, about 300 gallons of water per day for every citizen: in Britain today we use about 50 gallons each, per day. By the fourth century in Rome there were eleven public baths, 856 private baths, and 144 public lavatories flushed with water, as well as a large number of private ones.

The baths themselves had adopted the combination of steaming and massage which had come from India, and which is still the characteristic of the 'Turkish bath'. A bell would ring about one o'clock to inform intending bathers that the water was hot, and after this customers would drift into the baths, paying a quarter of an *as*. They undressed in the *apodyterium*, and were rubbed by slaves with oil and water, or, if they were covered with road dust from a long journey, with a mixture of African sand and oil. Many of the more fastidious customers brought their own specially perfumed oil with them. Anointed, they moved into the hot room, or *calidarium*, to sweat and gossip, or they could, if actively inclined, play athletic games in the *sphaeristerium* before proceeding to the hot room. When the masseur was ready, they went into the *laconicum*, a steam room arranged just over the hypocaust or furnace: water was poured over the bathers and they were then massaged and scraped with *strigils*, bronze tools looking rather like curved gouges, with grooves to collect the mixture of oil, dirt, and dead skin that always becomes loosened in a steam room. After this massage and cleansing they were sponged, oiled again, and took a plunge into the *frigidarium*, a large open-air swimming bath in the centre of one of the rooms. A *tepidarium*, or warm room, heated with the hot air from the furnace passed through hollow bricks, formed a general meeting-place and vestibule: in the great imperial baths there were also rooms for dining, for lectures and meetings, and gardens to walk in between baths or meals. In early Rome the baths were strictly for men, then special times were set aside for women, and latterly, among other features of the Decline, men and women congregated together in the baths. This soon led to other uses for the buildings, and in the Street of the Fullers in Pompeii an advertisement can still be read, the work of some early property agent:

A Social History as Seen Through the Uses and Abuses of Dirt

IN PRAEDIS . JULIAE . SP.F. FELICIS LOCANTUR
BALNEUM . VENEREUM . ET. NONGENTUM . PERGULAE
CENACULA . EX . IDIBUS . AUG . PRIORIS . IN . IDUS.
AUG . SEXTAS . ANNOS. CONTINUOS . QUINQUE
S . Q . D . L . E . N . C.

which has been translated as 'On the estate of Julia Felix, daughter of Spurius Felix, are to be let from the 1st to the 6th of the Ides of August, on a lease of five years, a bath, a brothel, and 90 shops, bowers, and upper rooms.' Arguments still go on among scholars about the initials at the end. Obviously they stood for something as familiar as the '2 rec. 4 bed. oil-f c.-h. gar 2 c, lge gdn' of our modern estate agents' advertisements, but what that familiar something was is now lost. One scholar has suggested that they mean 'not to be let to anyone practising an infamous profession', but in that case one can only presume that running a *venereum* did not count. The baths that remain visible in the excavations at Pompeii, the Stabaean Baths, share with many other features of that city the eerie feeling of a town not dead, but only asleep. One can imagine bathers coming in at any time to fold their clothes and put them carefully away in the square stone lockers of the *apodyterium*.

Wherever the Romans went, they built baths, from Africa to Hadrian's Wall. Delighted by the discovery of naturally warm water, they built baths at *Aquae Sulis*, now known as Bath, within ten years of occupying Britain, and the Great Bath, 80 feet long and 40 feet wide, is still fed from a lead conduit made by some Roman plumber nearly 2000 years ago. There are remains of small baths in many parts of the country, and the excavations of a fine set of buildings, almost on the metropolitan Roman scale, at *Uriconium* (Wroxeter) near Shrewsbury: many of the wares sold in the near-by shops were found during the excavations, and Shrewsbury Museum has therefore a very fine collection of Roman-style household goods. At Newstead, a 'police' post north of Hadrian's Wall, there is a small bath with facilities for heating the water, and at Housesteads Fort, on the wall itself, there are still remains of stone water-tanks, drains, a bath-house, and a suite of small bathrooms in the barracks. Baths in private houses were rare, because of the availability of public baths in so many towns, but in some of the larger and more isolated villas there were smaller versions of the public baths, complete with hypocaust, steam rooms, and pool. To cope with all the plumbing required, pipes were made in earthenware, lead, or occasionally wood, although wood was frowned upon because of its tendency to warp and leak. (Among so many arts practised by the Romans, the art of making good water pipes was lost for 1700 years. Wooden pipes were used, despite their tremendous rate of leakage, up to 1800.) The lead pipes at Bath are made in oblong section, and turned over at the seams in the manner still recognized by good craftsmen in lead. At Silchester there was a pump for raising the water, made of wood with a lead cylinder-lining. It appears to have been built using a design given by Vitruvius in the first century.

The men who constructed and used the baths, water-tanks, pumps, and all the apparatus of cleanliness, were no sybaritic idlers, whatever their 'betters' in Rome may have been. The crack troops had marched from Rome and Northern Italy through the whole of France, crossed the Channel in tiny boats, and marched all the long miles up to Northumberland, always ready to fight off angry swarms of British or to put an end, peacefully or otherwise, to inter-tribal warfare. 'The soldiers were diligently instructed to march, to run, to leap, to swim, to carry heavy burdens, to handle every species of arms that was used either for offence or for defence, either in distant engagement or in a closer onset; to form a variety of evolutions; and to move to the sound of flutes in the Pyrrhic or martial dance,' says Gibbon. Such troops were the men who conquered, and occupied, about sixteen hundred square miles of the world, bringing order and cleanliness wherever they travelled.

Cleanliness and urbanity go together. The Romans were clean mainly because they set great value on public and collective life: if a man is going to spend most of his time talking, debating, working, in close proximity to other people, he can do this with more grace and less distraction if the smell and appearance of his face and body do not offend his neighbours. This same urbanity and interest in social life was anathema to the rising cult of the Christians, who were firmly convinced that the things of this world were vanities, and they tended to reject all the other Roman values, including cleanliness, along with the theological ones. 'They seriously renounced the business and the pleasures of the age; abjured the use of wine, of flesh, and of marriage; chastised their body, mortified their affections, and embraced a life of misery, as the price of eternal happiness,' remarks Gibbon, picking over the wretched habits of the early Christians with the formidable scalpel of his prose. '. . . It was the practice of the monks either to cut or shave their hair; they wrapped their heads in a cowl, to escape the sight of profane objects; their legs and feet were naked, except in the extreme cold of winter; and their slow and feeble steps were supported by a long staff. The aspect of a genuine anachoret was horrid and disgusting: every sensation that is offensive to man was thought acceptable to God; and the angelic rule of Tabenne condemned the salutary custom of bathing the limbs in water, and of anointing them with oil.' Athanasius, in his life of Antony of Thebais, an illiterate youth who became founder of one of the anchorite sects, remarks with approval that Antony had a holy horror of clean water, and his feet in particular were never contaminated by it, except by accident. St. Benedict, one of the greatest administrators of the early church, pronounced solemnly that 'to those that are well, and especially to the young, bathing shall seldom be permitted', and his followers accepted the prohibition with great zeal. St. Agnes was never washed throughout her lifetime (the fact that the lifetime was only thirteen years may have had some connection with this), and a fourth-century pilgrim to Jerusalem boasted that she had not washed her face for eighteen years so as not to disturb the holy water used at her baptism. St. Jerome criticized some of his followers for keeping too clean. Many of the ascetics went further than simple neglect of their own bodies, and sought out lepers, sufferers from ulcers, and other people with the more disgusting and dirty diseases, so as to give the ascetic the chance to wash ulcered feet with his own hair, in the style of St. Mary Magdalene, to kiss leprous or ulcered skin, and generally wallow in the perverse delights of coprophilia. It is a pity that they did not try, while giving themselves such strange enjoyment, to use any practical means of relieving the suffering of the patients. St. Hugh of Lincoln used to gather together a great assembly of male lepers, and then kiss them, reserving his fondest and closest embraces for those who were most deformed, and taking care to kiss the actual ulcers on their skin. Dr.

Creighton, a nineteenth-century medical historian who quotes this odd habit, adds that St. Hugh's practices 'must have come as a not altogether agreeable surprise to men who already had sufficient physical discomfort to contend with'.

Queen Matilda, according to Dr. Creighton, surprised her brother David by her unusual devotions:

> When he was serving as a youth at the English court, one evening he was with his companions in the lodgings, when the Queen called him to her chamber. He found the place full of lepers, and the queen standing in the midst with her robe laid aside and a towel girt round her. Having filled a basin with water, she proceeded to wash the feet of the lepers and to wipe them with the towel, and then taking them in both her hands, she kissed them with devotion.
>
> To whom her brother: 'What dost thou, my lady? Certes if the king were to know this, never would he deign to kiss with his lips that mouth of thine polluted with the soil of leprous feet.'
>
> But she answered with a smile: 'Who does not know that the feet of an Eternal King are to be preferred to the lips of a mortal king? See, then, dearest brother, wherefore I have called thee, that thou mayest learn by my example to do so also.'

It does not appear that David profited by the lesson.

Leprosy had come from Egypt with the Roman soldiers, a more permanent prize than Cleopatra. It appeared as a skin complaint in which small patches of the skin seemed to lose all feeling, so that pins could be stuck into them without any sensation of pain. The spots turned pale grey or white, and larger areas of the body began to suffer from the same anæsthesia. Then some of the patches turned into sores, and eventually large open ulcers, producing a continuous stream of pus. The hands and feet became deformed and sponge-like, and the nose was often affected, so that continuous sneezing and finally suffocation resulted. It was a disease aptly called 'the living death'.

As leprosy spread slowly through the Mediterranean area (for, despite its fearsome reputation, it is not very contagious), northern Europe remained mercifully ignorant of the disease except as something mentioned in the Bible, but the Crusades brought Europeans from all countries into Palestine, one of the great endemic centres of leprosy. Many a returned warrior, musing over the strange sunlit landscape and the exotic luxuries of the Arabs, must have felt a peculiar deadness in the hand—perhaps when he clutched a sword hilt or a horse's rein —and realized, with a sudden chill, that the words of Leviticus could be applied to *him*:

'And the leper in whom the plague is, his clothes shall be rent, and his head bare, and he shall put a covering upon his upper lip, and shall cry, Unclean, unclean. All the days wherein the plague shall be in him he shall be defiled; he is unclean: he shall dwell alone; without the camp shall his habitation be.'

It seemed inconceivable to the medieval mind that Crusaders of all people could have done anything deserving of Divine punishment, and many of the 'new lepers' were a little too powerful to be whipped away from the city boundaries, which had been the standard Old Testament treatment meted out in Italy to lepers. The old notion that leprosy was something like venereal disease, a just reward for sin, suddenly appeared wildly out of date.

Fortunately, the Church can always find unassailable arguments for any policy which it seems expedient to follow. The Old Testament was forgotten, and the New Testament provided the answer. Christ himself had eaten in the house of Simon the Leper, and had cured a leper in 'a certain city': obviously leprosy was not a punishment for sin, but a mark of divine grace. Even more ingenious commentators deduced that the passage in Isaiah: 'vere languores nostros ipse tulit, et dolores nostros ipse portavit et reputavimus eum quasi leprosum, percussum a Deo et humilitatum', which had up to now been used as authority to banish lepers from the company of society, was really a prophecy that Christ would be 'treated like a leper' or even that he might have been a leper in fact. Leprosy suddenly became respectable, and many of the faithful set up leper hospitals to care for the unfortunate bearers of the divine stigma. The first English hospital was in Nottingham, but they soon began to spring up all over England.

Leper-hospitals, or lazar-houses, became the fashionable way of purchasing one's way to Heaven, and the supply soon began to exceed the demand. There were at one time nearly three hundred in England and two thousand in France, thrown up in an atmosphere of religious mania. These were often tended by friars and other religious men trained in the best traditions of St. Benedict, so they were by no means the hygienic places that the word 'hospital' suggests today, but rather insanitary holes suitable for the poor to die in.

Monasteries were also endowed richly, but were very little more clean. Fresh straw for the mattresses was provided once a year: water for baths 'two, three, or even four times a year' says an eleventh-century chronicler. Many had drains of a sort, and often these were tunnels which served two or more buildings—hence the tunnels which, to the delight of the anti-clerical or romantically minded, seem to connect monasteries with near-by nunneries. Obviously access could be had from one to the other through the sewer, but it would have taken quite a lot of the amorous charm out of the situation. In an excavation in St. Albans, A. J. Lamb writes:

'Here was found a deep pit, 18 ft. 8 in. long by 5 ft. 3 in. wide; the walls were 15 in. thick. The depth of the pit below the Cloister floor level was 25 ft. At the bottom were found pieces of pottery and fragments of coarse cloth which, it is thought, were old gowns torn up by the monks and used as toilet paper. Evidence, too, that the monks suffered from digestive troubles, which were by no means rare in those days, was proved by the finding in the pit, seeds of the buckthorn—a powerful aperient.'

Such an elaborate privy was unusual, in fact, the Abbot who built this 'Necessary house' refers to it with pride: 'none can be found more beautiful or more sumptuous'.

Most of the monks still retained the habits and outlook of Gibbon's anachorets and were contemptuous of cleanliness. Their robes were issued so rarely, in most monasteries, that there cannot often have been old ones to use as toilet paper, as at St. Albans, and as they lived, ate, and slept in them, the odour of sanctity must have been somewhat overpowering. The Roman baths fell down, and the Christian abbeys and churches rose up; the spiritual gain may have been there, but there was an Apocalypse to come.

3. *The Dance of Death*

'In the two and twentieth yeare of his Raigne, a contagious Pestilence arose in the East and South parts of the world, and spreade it selfe over all Christendome; and comming at last into *England*, it so wasted the people, that scarce the tenth person of all sorts was left alive. There dieth in *London* (some say in *Norwich*) between the first of January, and the first of July, 57374 persons. . . .'

Thus Sir Richard Baker, in his *Chronicle* of English history from the beginnings of time up to that flower of humanity, Charles I, summarizes and dismisses the Black Death as a 'casualty' of the reign of Edward III, together with monstrous fishes, seen in the Thames and elsewhere, unusual births, and ominous stars seen in the eastern sky. Sir Richard may claim to be the first social historian as he prides himself, in his introduction to the *Chronicle*, on including such *meaner accidents* of history as the Black Death, as well as matters of state. There is, for the modern reader, a curious contrast between the exactitude of the figures and the vagueness about the place, but it has the detached air of the true statistician.

Contemporaries of the Black Death were less detached. 'O happy posterity, who will not experience such abysmal woe and will look on our testimony as a fable,' lamented Petrarch, as the population of Florence perished miserably around him. 'We see death coming into our midst like black smoke, a plague which cuts off the young, a rootless phantom which has no mercy for fair countenance,' wrote the Welsh poet Jeuan Gathin as the horror spread inexorably westwards.

15

The symbolic *blackness* of the plague deeply impressed those who watched its progress. For a short time in France it was called *la mort bleue*, because of the septicaemic blue bruises on the skin in the later stages, but universally it earned its sombre names, the Black Death, *la peste noire, der schwarze Tod*: it was swift, appallingly infectious, and seemed designed by a malign Providence to make death not only terrifying, but demoralizing and disgusting to the utmost degree. The living body began to rot before death came to finish the process.

'. . . all the matter which exuded from their bodies let off an unbearable stench; sweat, excrement, spittle, breath, so foetid as to be overpowering; urine turbid, thick, black or red . . .'*

Boccaccio, in the introduction to the *Decameron*, describes the disease from which his aristocratic story-tellers had shut themselves away. 'It began in both men and women with certain swellings in the groin or under the armpit. They grew in the size of a small apple or egg, more or less, and were vulgarly called tumours (*gavoccioli*). In a short space of time these tumours spread from the two points named all over the body. Soon after this the symptoms changed and black and purple spots appeared on the arms or thighs or any other part of the body, sometimes a few large ones, sometimes many little ones. These spots were a certain sign of death, just as the original tumour had been and still remained.'

The *gavocciolo* is the bubo or boil that gives the name to the Black Death and similar pestilences—bubonic plague. The pain of the buboes was often intolerable, as the lymphatic glands in the underarm, groin, or neck suppurated and swelled. '. . . it is seething, terrible, wherever it may come, a head that gives pain and causes a loud cry, a burden carried under the arm, a painful angry knob, a white lump. It is of the form of an apple, like the head of an onion, a small boil that spares no one. Great is its seething, like a burning cinder . . .' says Jeuan Gathin. As late as 1845 Francis Galton, travelling in the Near East, noted that the quarantine officers in Beirut had a rough-and-ready but effective test for plague carriers—a light tap under the armpit. Those who could keep an unruffled calm were allowed through, while those with even the beginnings of a *gavocciolo* were sure to wince.

* J. P. Papon, *Époques mémorables de ce Fléau*, 1800.

The black or blue spots, the 'tokens', were smaller boils or patches of gangrened flesh, coloured like a bruise where the blood had escaped under the skin. They occurred on the skin in patterns, following the lines of the lymphatic system underneath, and were regarded, not unreasonably, as the special marks of the angel of death. Some English parish registers form a macabre memorial to the 'tokens', as the vicars have used the patterns of dots as a sign of plague, in the burial registers— perhaps the word itself seemed too dreadful to write. Usually sufferers died three to four days after the appearance of the tokens, but in the Black Death there was a more deadly form of plague, pneumonic plague, which attacked the lungs and caused death in as little as twenty-four hours, from the first signs of the tokens to the final collapse. It was also more infectious, as the breath from one victim was enough to transmit the disease to others: in the crowded medieval cities pneumonic plague spread like fire in dry bracken.

Plague is still a mystery disease, still difficult to cure, and still terrifying. It is sudden, lethal, and horrible in its symptoms, reducing its victims to a stinking carrion even before they are dead. It seems to ebb and flow across the world like a destroying tide. The earliest records show plague coming from the east— China, Russia, Mongolia—reaching Egypt in A.D. 542, travelling across Europe and reaching England around 600, the Wales of Cadwallon about twenty years later, and Ireland in 664. Bede records a wave of pestilences around this time, and in his description of the death of the saintly Queen Etheldreda in 660, he emphasizes the 'tumour' full of poisonous matter which developed in her neck.

The disease seems to have receded in Europe until the Black Death, which started again in Central Asia—Semiriechinsk, according to the researches of the Russian archaeologist Chwolson—in 1338-9, and again spread westwards. It travelled through the Mediterranean countries swiftly, and was brought to England in 1348.

'In the year 1348, in Melcombe, in the county of Dorset, a little before the Feast of St. John the Baptist, two ships, one of them from Bristol, came alongside. One of the sailors had brought with him from Gascony the seeds of that terrible pestilence, and, through him, the men of that town of Melcombe were the first in England to be infected.' The grey friars of Lynn recorded a melancholy claim to fame for Melcombe, now part of Weymouth, which modern inhabitants accept as part of their heritage: it seems likely that there were several ports which received the plague almost simultaneously, as there was a constant coming and going of knights and their retainers to France. Edward III was indulging in his favourite sport, which we dignify as the Hundred Years War, and his knights owed him so many days' 'knight service' per year; all the southern ports must have seen the knights and their men setting out to serve their time, and coming back a few weeks later with booty, strange oaths, and the plague. Bristol and Southampton also claim to be the first towns to suffer the Black Death: no doubt there are descendants of Christopher Columbus's crew who look back proudly on their ancestor who brought syphilis to Europe.

Plague spread rapidly in England, and was recorded in the north by 1349, and past Aberdeen by the end of that year. It waxed and waned, reappearing in 1361–2 in a form almost as deadly as the Black Death, then in large epidemics in 1368–9, 1375, 1390–1, 1406–7, 1464, 1479, 1500, 1513, 1563, 1569, 1593, 1610, 1625, and the famous Great Plague of 1665: it never really died out during these years, and parish registers record deaths from plague practically every year from around 1540, when the registers mostly begin, to 1670–80. The Great Plague was not the end of plague in England, but its last serious blow: in Europe it continued longer, and Vienna had to wait until 1714 before the Emperor could order a medal with the words '*Wien ohne Weh*' (Vienna free from woe).

A third great outbreak of plague started in Yunnan in 1892, reached India in 1896 and killed about six million people in that sub-continent alone, travelled through Europe with diminishing power, and killed a few people in Suffolk in 1910. It is still endemic in parts of Africa, and the chances of recovery, even with modern medical resources, are still rather low, so our quarantine officers do well to remember that *quarantine* means the period of *forty* days decreed long ago in Florence as the period that strangers must wait before entering the city: typically of medieval thinking, this was not a period of time decided upon by observation of the plague, but the period of time spent by Our Lord in the wilderness.

To the ecologist, the whole process must seem like that of bacteria becoming immune to an antibiotic, or insects resistant to an insecticide. The plague germ, *Pasteurella pestis*, has a period of success against humankind, until it reaches a core of resistant people; then there is a lull during which the resistant humans multiply. The bacteria become almost powerless for a while, and plague recedes, and then some slight alteration in the germ, or the birth of a few generations of humans who have not been exposed to the disease, gives the germ another chance of success.

Plague is carried by fleas, which in their turn are passengers on rats and other rodents. *Xenopsylla cheopis*, the flea mostly concerned, is harboured by marmots in Central Asia, and then transfers to rats in the Western countries. The rats themselves are susceptible to plague, and this may be one of the reasons why epidemics finally fade out, but the fleas can spread to human beings or other animals and pass from one victim to another, taking a little blood and paying for it in a deadly currency of plague germs. It is ironic that, without the flea as a go-between, bubonic plague is not really very infectious: it requires very close contact with the sick person for the germs to transfer. While the frightened medieval citizens and the baffled doctors were devising elaborate defences against the 'miasma' of plague, against breathing the same air as the plague victims, or smelling them, and even against the supposed malignant powers of the sufferer's eyes, they still allowed their houses to run with rats and their bodies and beds with fleas. Fleas were so common that they were regarded almost affectionately as a constant companion to man—certainly fleas and lice, if not man's *best* friends, might be considered his closest friends—and those who were lucky enough to have the best and warmest clothes often had the most fleas. When St. Thomas à Becket was disrobed for burial, after his assassination, a large population of disciples was evicted. 'The dead Archbishop was clothed in an extraordinary accumulation of garments. Outermost there was a large brown mantle; next, a white surplice; underneath this, a fur coat of lambs' wool; then a woollen pelisse; then another woollen pelisse; below this the black cowled robe of the Benedictine order; then a shirt; and finally, next to the body, a tight-fitting suit of coarse hair-cloth covered on the outside with linen, the first of its kind seen in England. The innumerable vermin which had infested the dead prelate were stimulated to such activity by the cold, that his hair-cloth, in the words of the chronicler, "boiled over with them like water in a simmering cauldron".* Friar Alberto in the second tale of the fourth day of the *Decameron*, sums up the ecclesiastical attitude to warm clothing—'I will do something today that I have not done for a very long time. I shall undress myself ...' St. Thomas, not so much concerned with amorous adventures, would no doubt have scorned such latin extravagances.

Not suspecting the humble flea, and knowing nothing of bacteria, contemporaries of the Black Death sought for the evil spirits, poisonous atmospheres, or deadly rays from comets that must have spread the disease. Martin Luther, during a later outburst of the plague, declared that evil spirits 'poisoned the air or otherwise infected the poor people by their breath and injected the mortal poison into their bodies'. Credulous observers reported a blue flame flying through the air and developing on the lips of the dying. In 1338 the plague was ascribed to the poisonous remains of a great infestation of locusts that appeared from the east and ravaged Italy and Germany—it was reported that the locusts settled so thickly on the thatched roofs of houses that their liquid excrement dripped through like a foul rain into the rooms below. Forestus Alcmarianos covers all the possibilities:

> Newly developed flies, worms, and midges are observed on the snow, the fruit and other crops fail to mature or rot, disease is observed particularly among sheep and swine, dogs go mad, many move like shadows on the wall, black vapours are observed to rise from the earth like a mist, the ravens are prompted by unusual impulses and fly around the hospitals in pairs. In the neighbourhood of water there is for a full hour a sound of washing and beating of clothes at night which is heard quite close, and it has been observed that this is indicative of a plague among women. Birds, contrary to their habits, are restless at night, fly about hither and thither, certain birds called plague birds appear, some maintain that a ghost with a voice like some lowing domestic animal is

* Sir William Macarthur.

20

heard, frogs sit huddled together in scores or one on top of the other, in the hospitals and sick houses a great rushing wind is heard, and when one perceives among men a great lack of reliability, jealousy, and hatred and wantonness, if then the plague does not ensue, some other inscrutable disease that is difficult to cure is sure to come.

With such a plethora of omens, one feels that only an ungrateful Providence would fail to come up with *some* disease: Forestus shows a talent for covering all his bets that would serve him well as a writer of astrological predictions.

Other signs of forthcoming plague were crosses on the skin, particularly on the hands and feet where Christ's stigmata occurred, and drops of blood found on bread taken from the oven. This last is not a fable, although it does not portend plague—there are certain types of fungus that can infect dough and produce blood-red drops or spots on the bread. They still find a use in the important Italian industry concerned with miraculous relics of saints' blood that never solidify.

In the face of overwhelming disaster, the thin veneer of rationality peels away from the human mind, to reveal the deep layers of irrational belief, superstition, symbolism—the layers that Jung called the 'Collective Unconscious'. When science cannot help, people turn to magic. Amulets were seized upon with desperation, and were produced in enormous numbers by businesslike magicians and quacks. The most popular was the ancient ABRACADABRA triangle, inscribed on parchment and rolled into various magical forms, but gems, herbs such as garlic and vervain, mass-produced 'unicorn's horn', and countless other materials were used. When it was obvious that the Christian prayers offered by the priests could not hold off the plague, many communities slipped back to older customs. The Wend peasants ploughed a protective furrow round their villages with a four-ox plough drawn by six naked virgins and a widow who had been seven years in widowhood—a custom which apparently persisted until about 1890 in the face of much disapproval from the Church. Many communities found a scapegoat—animal or human—heaped it with the clothes or other remnants of plague victims, and drove it out of the village, in the hopes that it would take the pestilence with it.

The flagellants, one of the most macabre developments of a nightmarish time, provided a kind of professional scapegoat service. Phillipus Dietz explains their motives and reasoning: '. . . if the body is to be restrained from lasciviousness and evil desires and trained to chastity and moderation, scourges, whips, discipline and cilicia [hair shirts or similar garments], and such like means and painful instruments, should be ready at hand. . .' Many people would have accepted the truth of this, but baulked at the actual application of scourges, whips, and painful instruments to their own persons. The flagellants offered them vicarious asceticism, travelling from town to town in a body, and putting on an open-air service during which the members of the fraternity flogged themselves until the blood ran. Henry of Herford describes the scourges: 'Each scourge was a kind of stick from which three tails with large knots hung down. Right through the knots iron spikes as sharp as needles were thrust which penetrated about the length of a grain of wheat or a little more beyond the knots. With such scourges they beat themselves on their naked bodies so that they became swollen and blue, the blood ran down to the ground and bespattered the walls of the churches in which they scourged themselves. Occasionally they drove the spikes so deep into the flesh that they could only be pulled out by a second wrench.'

The rules of the 'order' forbade the flagellants to bathe, to wash their heads, or to change their blood-soaked clothes, without special permission from the master of the group, so they must have presented a repellent picture. For the onlookers, however, they produced the mixture of horror and fascination that any thorough-going zealot can call upon: these filthy creatures torturing themselves, often to death, were at least trying to do something positive about the plague, when all that the local priest could offer was prayers and penances. The deaths of the flagellants—inevitable in any case from infected wounds —were occasion for extra self-punishment by the others. More lethal was the way in which they carried the plague from town to town as they went on their black pilgrimages.

Medicine was little better than magic. The 'cures' and prophylactics were based on fantastic flights of imagination and minimal practical experience (like much modern psycho-analytical writing). Paracelsus (Theophrastus Bombast von

Hohenheim), the great father of medical quackery, reported on the widespread use of dried toads to relieve the pain of the buboes, explaining that, as a live toad is moist and slimy, so a dead dried toad will absorb any moist and slimy material from the body: 'when it is full it should be thrown away and a new one applied; no one should feel disgusted at such a physic.' In such a time of trouble, no one could afford to be disgusted at even more repulsive practices. On an obscure reasoning that evil can drive out evil, the boils of dead plague victims were cut out and dried, and administered to the sick as a remedy; in East Prussia the peelings from the boils were given to the healthy in milk, as a prophylactic. The belief that one poison could drive out another induced many people, particularly the poor who could not afford doctors' bills, to spoon the pus out of the buboes of the dying and dead, and swallow it. St. Catherine of Siena is renowned for having subjugated the body by drinking a bowl of pus, but it may have been merely a mundane precaution against plague infection.

England had its share of all these magical and pseudo-medical practices, and one can imagine how each new 'cure', reported from the European countries, found an eager audience as news of the pestilence came from ever closer quarters. But all the efforts were in vain. When the Black Death struck, it carried away whole families, whole districts, in three to four days. Baker's figure of nine-tenths of the English population carried off is a serious over-estimate, but in some cities the proportion approached this level—in Bristol, for instance, it was said that only one-tenth of the citizens were left alive by 1349. There were no reliable population figures, so most of these chroniclers' figures must be guesswork. Baker's figure of 57,374 applies in fact to Norwich, the second city in the kingdom at this time, and this was out of 70,000 inhabitants before the plague. In London it was said that over 100,000 people perished. However, J. C. Russell in *British Mediaeval Population* gives good reasons for assessing the population of London in 1348 at only 60–70,000, and Norwich at 13,000.

Whatever the real figures, the losses were great enough to disrupt the medieval social system almost to breaking-point. As Robert of Avesbury said: '. . . This plague sweeping over the southern districts, destroyed numberless people in Dorset,

Devon and Somerset. . . . On account of the scarcity of labourers, women and even small children were to be seen with the plough.' Priests, if they tried to do even the least of their duties, were particularly liable to infection (and perhaps, like St. Thomas, they had warmer clothes and tended to attract more fleas) and the death-roll in the Church was catastrophic. Reasonably reliable figures can be drawn up for deaths in the priesthood, because most of the records of appointments to parishes still exist. About 25,000 priests died in England alone, and in one parish (Shaftesbury) there is a chilling reminder of the speed with which plague struck: new vicars were appointed on 29 November, 10 December, 6 January, and 12 May 1348–9, owing to the death of the incumbent. The Bishop of Bath and Wells, Ralph of Shrewsbury, writing from the relative safety of his country home in Wiveliscombe, was forced to sanction emergency measures that would have scandalized St. Paul, and underline the acute shortage of priests:

'. . . at once and publicly instruct and induce, yourselves or by some other, all who are sick of the present malady, or who shall happen to be taken ill, that *in articulo mortis*, if they are not able to obtain any priest, they should make their confession of their sins . . . even to a layman, and, if a man is not at hand, then to a woman.'

As the sick began to outnumber the well, the dead bodies became too numerous to dispose of with any of the traditional decencies. The funeral service and burial degenerated into a hasty shovelling into plague pits on the outskirts of each town or village. Gravediggers and carters to carry the corpses could only be recruited from the class with nothing to lose, criminals, vagabonds, and beggars, and they made the best use of their opportunities to rob not only the corpses, but any house into which the sickness had penetrated, knowing well that no neighbours or officials would dare to enter such a house to interfere. These ghouls soon became almost as much an object of fear as the plague itself. They were reputed in particular to rape any moderately attractive females in the stricken houses, whether alive, dying, or already dead, and terrifying stories of this are retailed by most of the authors on plague, with a conscientiously shocked tone. In view of the disgusting state of the bodies of plague victims, the tales seem unlikely: what is probable is that the grave-carriers stripped the bodies of any reasonably well-to-do women, because of their expensive petticoats and other clothes. This would be seen as sufficiently depraved and sacrilegious to start a flock of atrocity stories in the medieval towns.

Ravens and kites flew over the streets, and half-wild dogs roamed the cities, getting their sustenance by gnawing the corpses that remained unburied. Those people who had so far escaped the plague shut their doors against possible carriers and the threats of the burial gangs, so that many poor wretches died in the streets of the disease, or even of starvation and exposure, practically under the windows of their neighbours. It was indeed a time to stay indoors and look after one's own.

Many people fumigated their houses, or kept enormous fires burning, to drive the plague away. They burnt incense, juniper, laurel leaves, cypress, pine, balm, rosemary, lavender—anything to cover up the fearful stench in the streets. Plague waters were invented at various times, to pour on handkerchiefs or into pomanders (traditionally a dried orange filled with fragrant oils) for those who had to venture out: the original Eau de Cologne was in fact invented as a specific against plague, and uses a large proportion of oil of rosemary and similar herbal oils with a reputation for healing or prophylaxis. On the other hand, with the curious double-think that afflicts a community faced with a crushing disaster, it was also believed that other *foul* smells could keep away the plague and its attendant reek, and many householders spent their time crouched grotesquely over their privies inhaling the fumes. Alternatively the family or the patient would share their bed with a goat: the worse the smell of the goat, the better their chances of escaping alive from the plague. (M. R. Taylor, in the journal *Folk-Lore*, volume 40, 1929, reports that in Norfolk, up to that time, there was a belief that whooping-cough could be cured by holding the child head-downwards in the privy. This had to be the genuine stinking earth-closet, not a water-closet.)

When the plague abated, the lucky survivors came out of hiding, left their privies and their goats, and found a new world around them. The appalling death rate and the shortage of labourers had made the surviving able-bodied men far more valuable to landowners, and for the first time in centuries, the workers were in a position, if not to bargain for their labour, at least to offer it in a sellers' market. There were attempts to limit the rise in wage rates by law (the Ordinance and Statute of Labourers, 1349 and 1351) but in practice it was impossible for the lords to find enough labourers without paying higher wages than the statutory ones. The villeins who had been shackled to their own feudal lord and their own parish suddenly found opportunities to escape and make a new life. Some went to the towns, which had been depopulated to a worse degree than the country, and some found new employers—landowners, desperate for labour, did not enquire too closely whether a man had leave from his previous lord. Even so there were too few labourers to cope with the inefficient agriculture of the time, and many landowners changed over from crops to the pasturage of sheep and cattle, which needed fewer men to tend them. In towns, the few craftsmen and merchants who had survived found a ready market for any manufactured goods they could make or import, and rapidly made themselves rich, thus starting a new and fiercer phase in the long struggle between the landowners and the manufacturers.

The Black Death also taught one important moral or religious truth—all men are equal in the face of death. The pestilence, when it struck, carried away the priest and the lord as well as the peasant and the labourer: better housing, better clothes, and better food gave no protection, and even those rich people who shut themselves away, like Boccaccio's Pampinea and her companions, were not immune from the subtle penetration of the disease, the sudden chill finding of the tokens. . . . 'And one by one dropped the revellers in the blood-bedewed halls of their revel, and died each in the despairing posture of his fall,' says Poe, in 'The Masque of the Red Death'.

The terror and despair of the plague years has been immortalized, especially in Germany and eastern Europe, by depiction of 'The Dance of Death'—plague seen as a monstrous figure of death leading a mad and obscene dance over the countryside, and leaving behind a trail of corpses. The symbol had more meaning in Germany than in other countries, because of several outbreaks of St. Anthony's Fire among the population at the same time as the plague. St. Anthony's Fire is a type of ergotism, caused by a poisonous fungus growing on rye, and the main symptoms are delusions and dancing mania (the actual poison is closely related, chemically, to dextro-lysergic acid diethylamide, or LSD). It is possible, in fact, that the flagellants were suffering from St. Anthony's Fire when they embarked on their nightmare pilgrimage; in any case, the spread of the ergotism and the spread of plague occurred together to produce uniquely horrible scenes of madness and death.

The Dance of Death became one of the favourite subjects of German ecclesiastical artists, and the depictions of death are often masterpieces of the early grotesque romantic school, Death as the King of Terrors indeed! Perhaps it is just as well that the real cause of the Black Death remained unknown, for the sake of the artists at least. It would have been far more difficult to make a great universal symbol out of a flea.

*

Probably because of the peculiarly repulsive stench of plague victims, there began to be glimmerings of the idea that the filth in medieval houses and streets could have something to do with the spread of infection. There was a cursory attempt to clean up the worst of the city streets: the scavengers, or rakers, who had been appointed to 'remove all filth and take distresses, or else fourpence, from those who placed them there, the same being removed at their cost' were instructed to pursue offenders more actively, and the penalty rose to two shillings. These rakers had a thankless task, and in the rat-infested houses, full of rotten planks, often a dangerous one. Richard the Raker has passed into the annals of public health as an early martyr—he fell through the rotten planks of a public latrine and was drowned in the deep pit of excrement underneath.

London was going through one of its periodic crises of sewage disposal. In 1355 it was reported that the Fleet River, which should have been ten feet wide and 'deep enough to float a boat with a tun of wine', was choked by the filth of eleven latrines and three sewers that discharged into it. Cesspools, in theory and law, should have been at least 2½ feet from a neighbour's property if stone-lined, and 3½ feet away if not, but few people paid much attention to the regulations. In 1347 two men were prosecuted for piping ordure into a neighbour's cellar—it says a great deal about the general smell of London at the time that this economical device was not discovered until the cellar began to overflow.

Most of the rubbish eventually found its way into the Thames or the town ditch. This ditch, or moat, was first constructed in 1211, and was finished in 1213, as a defensive waterway 200 feet broad. It came up beside the Tower of London, northwards to Bishopsgate, and continued around the walls of the city. But it was not long before it became choked with rubbish, either accidentally or deliberately (many people adjoining the ditch saw the advantages of blocking it with rubbish so as to make gardens for their houses, and by 1598 it had ceased to be a useful waterway at all; gardens and even houses had been made along most of its length). There were occasional attempts to open the ditch up again: in 1354 it overflowed into the moat of the Tower of London, and Edward III ordered it to be cleared so as to re-establish the flow of water. It was cleansed again in 1379 by order of the mayor, John Philpot, at a cost of fivepence from every citizen, and Richard II established a toll or purchase tax on all goods sold by water or by land, towards repairing the city wall and clearing the ditch. In the end, however, private enterprise prevailed, and the banks were let out to building speculators who deliberately filled in the ditch so as to increase the size of their plots of land.

Human and animal dung and household rubbish, all discharged into the streets and left to find their own way to the river or the town ditch, were supplemented by the by-products of slaughtering and butchering. Many cattle were slaughtered in the St. Nicholas shambles, in Seacoal Lane. The meat that was not sold immediately would be preserved with coarse salt ('powder beef' because of the grains of salt, just as 'corned beef' is called after the corn-like grains of curing salt) and packed into tubs. St. Nicholas, after whom several slaughter-houses and shambles were named, was famous for having revived children who had been killed and salted down in a time of famine. After the meat had been prepared and sold, there was a residue of entrails and dung which was piled up on the edge of the Fleet River (now Farringdon Street) waiting for the rain to wash the rubbish into the water. Pigs were killed in Rother Street, otherwise known as Red Rose Street, and it was at last re-christened Pudding Lane, its modern title, because of the pigs' 'puddings' or entrails that were flung into it, to make their slow way down to the Thames at the bottom of the hill.

If conditions in the town streets were bad, conditions in the houses were very little better. In the country the very poor lived in tent-shaped huts made of mud and wattle around wooden posts, and the slightly better-off lived in wooden houses with two or three rooms. In either case, if the family owned any animals, these shared the accommodation. The anonymous author of *Gammer Gurton's Needle* has a great deal of robust fun when his characters are raking in the rubbish on the floor of the gammer's cottage, to find the lost needle. Instead of finding it, they pick up droppings from the chickens and the cat, a theatrical device that seems to have fallen out of use. As the old lady also has the swill bucket inside the room, the atmosphere can be imagined— indeed, the whole play serves to show how genteel our modern 'kitchen-sink' plays have become.

Sometimes the animals contributed even more to the atmosphere of the house: in Skelton's 'The Tunning of Elinour Rumming' Elinour's alehouse is depicted as overcrowded:

> ... With, 'Get me a staff,
> The swine eat my draff!
> They have drunk up my swilling-tub!'
> For, be there never so much press,
> These swine go to the high dais,
> The sow with her pigs,
> The boar his tail wrigs,
> His rump also he frigs
> Against the high bench!
> With 'Fo, there's a stench!
> Gather up, thou wench;
> Seeest thou not what is fall?
> Take up dirt and all,
> And bear out of the hall:
> God give it ill-preving,
> Cleanly as evil 'chieving!'
>
> But let us turn plain,
> There we left again.
> For, as ill a patch as that,
> The hens run in the mash-vat;
> For they go to roost

Straight over the ale-joust,
And dung, when it comes,
In the ale-tunnes.
Then Elinour taketh
The mash-bowl, and shaketh
The hen's dung away,
And skimmeth it into a tray
Whereas the yeast is,
With her mangy fistes:
And sometimes she blens
The dung of the hens
And the ale together,
And sayeth, 'Gossip, come hither,
This ale shall be thicker,
And flower the more quicker . . .'

It is, of course, perfectly true that hens' dung added to yeast would make the ale ferment, or 'flower' more quickly, but it is not a method that recommends itself.

Town-dwellers usually shared accommodation—apprentices and labourers lived with their masters. In Dekker's *The Shoemaker's Holiday* there is a vivid picture of Simon Eyre, the shoemaker, rousing his household:

'Where be these boys, these girls, these drabs, these scoundrels. They wallow in the fat brewis of my bounty, and lick up the crumbs of my table, yet will not rise to see my walks cleansed. Come out, you powder-beef queans! What, Nan! what, Madge Mumblecrust! Come out, you fat midriff-swag-belly-whores, and sweep me these kennels that the noisome stench offend not the noses of my neighbours. What, Firk, I say; what, Hodge! Open my shop-windows. . . .'

In any case, the possessions of the average family did not require much room. The vast inventories that have come down to us from noble families give an idea of the richness of life for, perhaps, one per cent of the population: the rest might own a chest, a table and some stools, a cauldron, wooden platters (which had begun to replace the simple notion of serving food on a trencher of bread by the early sixteenth century), knives, spoons (but no forks as yet) and straw palliasses to sleep on—bedsteads were rare luxuries.

Most buildings would be thoroughly blackened by wood

smoke, as many of them lacked chimneys of any kind, and those that existed were not efficient: 'Full sooty was hir bour, and eek hir halle,' says Chaucer of the poor widow in the 'Nun's Priest's Tale'. The smoke was expected to go out through a hole in the roof, but a large proportion of it did not. On the other hand, the dirt would not be readily visible, as windows were small or non-existent in most houses. So few people could read that there was little need for bright lighting, natural or otherwise, and window glass was expensive. Even in some of the richer houses, the windows were made of glass mounted in portable frames, so that they could be taken down when not needed, and windows without glass were kept small to avoid freezing draughts in winter. This general dim lighting and the blackened interiors of the houses must have made them pitch-black at night, whether moonlight or not, and this darkness provides the background for much of Chaucer's humour, as in the 'Reeve's Tale' when the miller's wife, depending only on her sense of touch, climbs into the wrong bed.

Lavatories, or garderobes (a curious medieval euphemism which has been revived in more modern times as 'cloakroom'), where they were constructed at all, were often placed on the upper floors of town houses, so that the hole was conveniently high above the pile of dung. Often garderobes projected from the house over the space between the side wall and that of the neighbouring house, so that the pile grew up neatly, out of the way of the front door but still accessible for clearing out from the street. Andreuccio, in the fifth tale of the second day of the *Decameron*, is tricked into one of these garderobes in a courtesan's house, and falls through the floor into the filth underneath:

'It was in a narrow space, such as we see between two houses, on two beams laid from one house to the other, with the place to sit down and a few planks, one of which had fallen down with him. . . .'

Some of the garderobes discharged into a convenient water-course, causing the kind of problem already mentioned in the case of the Fleet River: the monks of White Friars in Fleet Street complained that the smell from the Fleet River overcame all the frankincense burnt at their altars, and killed many of the brethren. There were public lavatories on London Bridge, among the houses and shops which were such a feature of the old bridge with its many arches, and at least one of these must have been large enough to have two doors; there is an account of an ingenious debtor who escaped his creditors by slipping out of the other door of the garderobe. Other garderobes actually discharged directly into the streets, and Ebbegate, a lane leading to the river from Thames Street, became virtually impassable because of the number of overhead hazards. In 1300, according to Stow, in his *Survey of London*, Sherborne Lane (near the church of St. Mary Abchurch) became popularly known as Shiteburn Lane.

In the larger buildings, especially those with defensive moats, the privies often led to the moat through channels cut in the walls. As an additional defence against intruders this no doubt had its advantages, but the effects of a hot summer on such a moat began to make the device unpopular. In some castles the drains were led away into the cellars and dungeons, and Marlowe, though cavalier with most of his facts, is probably correct in his description of the plight of Edward II in the dungeon of Berkeley Castle:

> This dungeon where they keep me is the sink
> Wherein the filth of all the castle falls.

Conditions were no worse in England than elsewhere in Europe. The problems of town life were becoming too complicated for the sanitary methods of the time. Ahead of his time in this, as in so much else, Leonardo da Vinci proposed New Towns, which would 'distribute the masses of humanity, who live crowded together like herds of goats, filling the air with stench and spreading the seeds of plague and death'. In these towns, sewage was to be carried away from public and private privies by underground sewers (a device totally unknown at the time or for centuries after, although it had been in use by the Romans of imperial days). He also proposed that the Château of Amboise, during the tenancy of Francis I, should have water-closets, with the channels for flushing water in the walls, and vent pipes to the roof. He even designed a lavatory seat arranged, by a counter-weight, to lift itself up when the sitter moved away—a hygienic device which has great attractions for lavatories used by both men and women, but curiously enough is to be found in the *women's* lavatories of County Hall in London. This is not presumably Leonardo's original design. His sanitary ideas, like his flying-machines, tanks, submarines, machine-guns, and other devices, remained buried in those incredible scribble-pads of genius, his Notebooks.

4. An Ounce of Civet

Leonardo also turned his attention to the bathroom; for the Corte Vecchia he designed a hot-water system with an apparatus for mixing hot and cold water, three parts hot water to four of cold, according to his Notebooks. In the case of the bath, however, he was not ahead of his time, but behind it—the hot bath was already beginning to decline in popularity by the time Leonardo became concerned with it.

The Crusaders had brought back many superficial features of Mohammedan civilization with them, as a small return for the wastage of men and resources in hopeless campaigns. Sugar and maize, cotton, muslin, and damask, glass mirrors, lemons and melons were some of the material things, while words we still use—chemistry, algebra, alcohol, tariff, corvette—are reminders of the pre-eminence of the medieval Arabs in the worlds of science, trade, and navigation. Among these refinements of life the Crusaders also brought back the idea of the hammām, the Turkish bath.

Baths had flourished in the Mohammedan civilization. The massage and cosmetic treatment traditional to Indian bathing were grafted on to the technical plumbing skill of the Roman Empire, to produce buildings and techniques that differ little from those in use today. The baths at Constantinople, typical of the larger installations, consist of a series of square rooms, carrying domes on pendentives. Each room is divided into a warm, hot, and steam area, corresponding to the *tepidarium*, *calidarium* and *laconicum* of the Roman imperial baths, together with dressing-rooms and rest rooms.

In the 'Story of Abū Kīr and Abū Sīr' in the *Thousand and One Nights* there is a detailed description of the ideal hammām. Abū Sīr, the barber, has come to a strange backward city with no baths, and obtains a grant from the king to build a hammām.

When the day came, Abū Sīr heated the hammām and the water in the basins, burnt incense and perfume in the braziers, and turned on the water of the fountain, which fell so sweetly that beside the tinkling of it all music would have been a discord. The large jet from the central basin was incomparably strange and would have turned aside the spirits of the blest. At length all within the hammām shone so bright and clean that the place surpassed the candours of lily and jasmine.

As soon as the King, with his wazīrs and amīrs, crossed the threshold of the great door, his senses were agreeably amazed; his eyes by the decoration, his nose by the perfumes, and his ears by the voices of the fountain. 'What is this?' he asked in surprise. 'It is a hammām,' answered Abū Sīr, 'but this is only the entrance.' He led the King into the first hall, and, causing him to mount the dais, undressed him and wrapped him from head to foot in suave towels. He put wooden bathing clogs upon his feet and introduced him to the second hall, where the Sultān sweated to a marvel. Then, with the help of the boys, he rubbed his limbs with hair gloves, so that all the inner dirt, accumulated by the pores of the skin, came forth in long threads like worms, much to the astonishment of the King. Then Abū Sīr washed him with plenty of water and soap and sent him down to the marble bath, which was filled with rose-scented water. After leaving him immersed for a certain time, he brought him forth and washed his head with rose-water and rare essences. Then he tinted the nails of his hands and feet with henna, which gave them a colour as of dawn. During these processes aloes and aromatic nard burnt about them and soaked them with soft vapour.*

The Europeans reproduced this atmosphere of luxury as well as they could, but in colder climates it was more difficult to

* *The Book of the Thousand Nights and One Night* (Fr. trans. Dr. J. C. Mardrus; Eng. trans. E. Powys Mathers), Routledge & Kegan Paul, 2nd ed. 1964.

provide the large quantities of hot water necessary for a really luxurious bath. The 'marble bath' tended to degenerate into a wooden tub, used in common by a great many customers, and presumably not emptied until they began to complain about the state of the water. The steam for the hot rooms was often provided from bakers' ovens, the bath backing on to the bakery, and the Bathmen's Guild sometimes came into conflict with ambitious members of the Bakers' Guild who tried to combine both businesses.

The sweating, which was such an important part of the bathing process, rapidly earned them the name of 'stews', whether they were public or private baths. The furnace of the King's *stywes* at Windsor was rebuilt in 1391, and there is an order to a carter to bring 229 pots to the castle from Farnborough, to facilitate carrying the water. At Eltham Palace John Jury the Potter supplied '120 pottes pro styuez' and Thomas the Mason was paid £4 for 'making the walls and setting 2 leads called fournaysez and 120 pottes for the stuuy house'. In a Westminster account book for 1325:

'. . . for 100 fagett for heating and drying the stuwes—3s. For a small barrell, 2 bokettes and a bowl for carrying water to the stuwes . . . carpenters working on the covering of the bathing tub and the partition in front of the said tub . . .' and similar details.

Mohammedan prejudices about the position of women, and particularly prohibitions against women showing any more of themselves than they need for navigation, made mixed bathing impossible in the truly Turkish bath—except in so far as a very rich man might bring male and female slaves to attend to him in a private bath. In Europe, on the other hand, there are numerous illustrations from the medieval period showing men and women sharing a tub, or bathers being attended by servants of the opposite sex. Not all of these pictures occur in romantic or amorous literature: some of them seem to depict social customs of the day. Unfortunately, like taking twilight walks with the Muses, this was a practice that led to abuses. Stews, bagnio, and bordello, which had signified only bathing-places (*bordello* merely means 'cabin' or 'room', referring to the various hot rooms in the baths), began to take their modern meanings.

> Where lately harbour'd many a famous whore,
> A purging bill, now fix'd upon the dore,
> Tells you it is a hot-house: So it ma',
> And still be a whore-house. Th'are *Synonima*.

says Ben Jonson, of a contemporary attempt to restore a stews to some sort of respectable reputation.

By the reign of Richard II the baths had become almost entirely brothels. William Walworth, several times mayor of London and a pillar of the Fishmongers' Company, also owned stews in Southwark—'The bordello, or Stewes, a place so called of certain stew-houses privileged there, for the repair of incontinent men to the like women . . .' says Stow. When Walworth was mayor in 1374 there were eighteen of these houses in Southwark alone, which no doubt added considerably to his income from selling fish. It also throws an interesting light on Walworth's great service for King Richard, for which he was knighted and is now famous—the killing of Wat Tyler during the Peasants' Revolt of 1381. According to Stow again:

'Also I find, that in the 4th of Richard II these stew-houses belonging to William Walworth, then mayor of London, were farmed by Froes of Flanders, and spoiled by Walter Tyler, and other rebels of Kent . . .'

The insurgents had burnt the prison in Southwark and attacked the bishop's palace in Lambeth, but damage to private property, especially valuable commercial property like brothels, was not to be tolerated. Walworth called up his fellow-merchants and their employees, and confronted Tyler and his followers. The young King, who was fourteen, rode out to temporize with the angry peasants, there were high words, and Walworth killed Tyler. The brothels were avenged.

Stow adds a curious footnote on the 'farming' or managing of the stews by Flemish 'froes': 'English people disdayned to be bawds. Froes of Flaunders were women for that purpose.' It is sad to think of the lack of management potential among the English women, who were, presumably, quite willing to be prostitutes, but not madams.

During the reign of Henry VIII the stews were closed altogether for a period:

Also if there be any house wherein is kept and holden any Hot-house or Sweating-house, for the Ease and Health of Men, to which be resorting or conversant and Strumpets, or Women of Evil Name or Fame. Or if there by any Hot-house or Sweating ordained for women, to the which is any common recourse of young Men, or other persons of evil Fame and Suspect Conditions. Also, if there be any such Persons that keep or hold any such Hot-houses, either for Men or Women, and have found not surety to the Chamberlain for their good and honest Behaviour, according to the laws of the City, and lodge any manner of person by Night, contrary to the Ordinance thereof made, by which he or they shall forfeit £20 to the Chamber, if they do the contrary.

However, the stews were revived again, and apparently at least one establishment for the legitimate purpose of bathing survived: Stow, who lists brothels as 'stew-houses', mentions one 'hot-house' still open in 1603. Soon after this, public bathing fell entirely into disuse, until the craze for spa bathing in the eighteenth century.

It has been suggested that the decline of the baths was due to their association with promiscuity and prostitution. It would, of course, be a credit to the human race if this were really the reason, but one looks in vain for any parallel situation in which a vicious institution has died out through lack of support. What seems more likely is that the crowding, heat, and dirty water encouraged the spread of disease, and after a time people began to notice the connection. It is significant that the baths probably reached their peak of popularity in England about the same time as the first great wave of plague in 1348–9, and gradually became less popular as successive following waves cut their swathes through the population. Lawrence Wright also suggests in his book *Clean and Decent*, reasonably enough, that as London and the other cities grew, the cost of transporting fuel to the baths gradually rose (although Southwark was very close to the 'country' even in 1600) and there was not, as yet, very much 'sea-coal' mined.

Whatever the reasons, bathing ceased. Europe had adopted a civilized custom from the east, adapted it, corrupted it, and

destroyed it. Little wonder that the Arabs and Turks regarded
Westerners as filthy in their habits.

'Glory be to Allāh, my child, that you have come safely out
of their hands. The people who now live in the city are
invaders from the black lands of the West' [says an old
gardener in the 'Tale of Kamar al-Zamān and Princess
Budūr']. 'They came up suddenly out of the sea one day and
massacred all the Faithful. They worship strange and
incomprehensible things, and speak an obscure and barbarous
language; they eat evil-smelling, putrescent things, such as
rotten cheese and game which they hang up; they never
wash, for, at their birth, ugly men in black garments pour
water over their heads, and this ablution, accompanied by
strange gestures, frees them from all obligation of washing
for the rest of their lives. That they might not be tempted by
water, they at once destroyed the hammāms and public
fountains, building in their places shops where harlots sell a
yellow liquid with foam on top, which they call drink, but
which is either fermented urine or something worse. And
their women, my son, are the abominations of calamity.
Like the men they do not wash, but they whiten their faces
with slaked lime and powdered eggshells. They do not wear
linen or drawers to protect them from the dust of the road,
so that their presence is pestilential and the fire of hell will
never clean them . . .'

For the great mass of medieval Westerners, all these criticisms
were only too true. The bath survived only in the ritual of the
Order of Chivalry, instituted by Henry IV at his Coronation
but never really organized until the reign of George I. The
candidate for the Order was placed under the care of 'two
esquires of honour grave and well-seen in courtliness and
nurture and also in feats of chivalry' who first made sure that
he was well-groomed by ordering a barber to shave him and cut
his hair. He was then led to a bath which had hangings, within
and without, of linen. (This idea of lining a bath was very
necessary when the tubs were made of stone and the supply of
hot water was limited. Those who today are discomfited by the
extraordinary chill which a cast-iron bath can retain, even after
the hot water has been run into it, may sympathize with

Margeurite of Flanders, who, in 1403, ordered 64 ells of 'common cloth' to pad two bath tubs. The modern Flemish ell is ¾ yard, so assuming a similar length in medieval times, this bath lining would take 48 yards of cloth.) The esquires undressed the candidate and put him in the bath, after which two ancient and grave knights came to lecture him on the duties of the Order and the responsibilities of knighthood in general, finally pouring water over him (it is not clear whether there was water in the bath from the first, or whether the candidate merely sat in the empty tub for his schooling, chilly but dry). Following the lectures, the candidate was taken to a bed and left to dry, then dressed in a hermit's robe, taken to the chapel, and left to keep his vigil of arms. The accolade followed on the next day.

As an aid to solemnity of thought, nothing could be more effective, one imagines, than sitting naked in a chilly bath and being lectured on the duties and responsibilities of chivalry, but considered as a piece of aversion therapy, it must have put many Knights of the Bath off the idea of actually bathing for the rest of their lives.

They washed their *hands*, of course. Forks being unknown, all food was eaten with the fingers from a common dish in the centre of the table; anything that could not be taken straight to the mouth was placed on a slice of bread which served as a plate. (The word *trencher* comes from Normal-French *tranchoir*, a slice. The modern French equivalent is *tranche*.) Chaucer's Prioress is credited with good table manners:

> At mete wel y-taught was she with-alle;
> She leet no morsel from hir lippes falle,
> Ne wette hir fyngres in hir sauce depe.
> Wel koude she carie a morsel and wel kepe,
> That no drope he fille upon hir breste;
> In curteisie was set ful much hir leste.
> Hire over-lippe wyped she so clene,
> That in hir coppe ther was no ferthying sene
> Of grece, whan she dronken hadde hir draughte.

This communal dipping meant, naturally, that hands needed to be washed before and after a meal: after, for obvious reasons, and before, because most people have an irrational dislike for eating other people's dirt. Basins were placed on the table between each pair of diners, and water poured over the hands from a jug. These jugs and basins were manufactured and decorated according to the status of the owner: they were an ideal vehicle for ostentation. Mere gentlemen used brass or pewter: such sets are occasionally mentioned in wills among the other household utensils. (Detailed lists of furniture and household goods are common in early wills: even the well-to-do had so few possessions, by our standards, that they could draw up a complete disposition of them without using too much parchment.) The nobility had gold, silver, or silver-gilt; the Duke of Anjou, in 1365, had an inventory of sixty sets in various precious metals. In the greatest houses servants called *ewers* (because they carried *eau*: the name has now passed down to the jug used for carrying the water) knelt before the guest with two basins, one full of scented water, and the other for the guest to hold his hands over while water was poured on them. In convivial parties guests might wash their neighbours' hands, especially if their neighbours were attractive women.

Even after this washing, table manners and hygiene were not appealing, and Alexander Barclay, the Scottish satirist, has some sharp things to say about conditions even at court:

> Coridon in court I tell thee by my soul
> For most part thou must drink of a common bowl,
> And where greasy lips and slimy beard
> Have late been dipped to make some mad afeard ...
> ... Through many hands shall pass the piece or cup,
> Before it comes to thee is all drunk up,
> And then if a drop or two therein remain
> To lick the vessel sometime thou art full fain ...*

The *Boke of Curtasye* offers the following advice on table manners:

> If thou spit on the borde or elles opene,
> Thou shalle be holden an uncurtayse mon ...

Cleaning your teeth with the tablecloth was another 'uncurtayse' habit to be avoided.

In poorer homes, of course, such refinements were unknown and unnecessary. The food was simpler—most people subsisted

* Modernized text by Edward Lucie-Smith.

on bread, cheese, whey or small beer, and a few relishes such as onions or garlic. Meat was only an occasional food for the mass of the people, and many of them had little or no means of cooking, so even stews or gruels were difficult to prepare. Such a diet does not leave the hands sticky or even very greasy, so the elaborate hand-washing ceremonies did not move down the social scale.

Even in the great houses, the ewers did not bring soap. In medieval times, and in fact up to the time of Queen Anne, soap was far too unpleasant to be introduced into the dining-room, and best kept away from the skin as well. Soap-making depends on fats and alkali, and the quality of both was very poor, although the basic process was the same as that in use today.

In making soap, fats and oils are heated with alkali: this changes the fat into soap and glycerine. The quality of the soap depends on the quality of the fat—dark or evil-smelling fat makes dark or evil-smelling soap, rancid fat makes rancid soap —and on the alkali. The only fats and oils available to the medieval soap-maker were tallow, from cattle and sheep, train-oil, made by boiling the oil from whale and seal blubber (the Dutch fishermen called it *traenoel*, from the word for tears or exudations) and occasionally olive oil from Spain, although the supply of this depended on relations with the Spanish kings. The only alkali was crude potash made from wood ashes and similar materials. (The modern chemists' name for the metal potassium is a Latinism coined by Sir Humphry Davy from pot-ash, the alkali obtained by boiling wood ashes in pots: the chemical symbol is K from *kalium*, the older name, which derives directly from Arabic *qalīy*—wood ashes—as does the word *alkali*—another reminder of the chemical skill of the medieval Arabs.) The best potash was made by burning seaweed, and so-called 'soap ashes' were produced in many seaports and carried inland; when made properly, these soap ashes were almost white.

With these resources, the soap-makers produced four grades of soap: 'castile' soap, made with olive oil and best soap ashes, which was rather soft and inclined to turn rancid, but just about usable on the skin; white soap, made with tallow and soap ashes, grey soap, made with tallow and ordinary wood-ashes; and black soap, made with stinking train-oil and wood ashes. Even now whale oil is difficult to turn into soap, except the crudest industrial material, because of its penetrating fishy smell and dark colour: the medieval black soap must have looked like tar and smelled like fish manure.

Many people made their own soap from dripping and similar kitchen fats, buying soap ashes or using their own wood ash as the alkali, but the difficulties of getting exactly the right balance of fat and alkali must have caused a few catastrophes. Too much fat makes the soap turn rancid in a matter of days, while too much alkali can take the skin off the user's hands. According to Stow, commercial soap-makers therefore set up to supply, if not a good product, a standard one:

'I have not read or heard of soap-making in this city (*London*) till within this fourscore years; that John Lane, dwelling in Grasse Street, set up a boiling-house for this city, of former time, was served of white soap in hard cakes (called Castell soap, and other) from beyond the seas, and of grey soap, speckled with white, very sweet and good, from Bristow, sold here for a penny the pound, and never above a penny farthing, and black soap for a halfpenny the pound.' Stow is wrong about the period when soap-making in London started; there are records of soap-makers in Sopar's Lane from 1259 at least. It is always difficult to calculate the real cost of goods in earlier periods, but a fair idea of the soap prices can be obtained by comparing them with prices of other necessities: in 1562, when the Ancaster MSS accounts record '4 lb of grey soap, 12d', a pig cost 6d and eggs were 2d a dozen. A farm-labourer's wages for the day would just about buy a pound of soap. Needless to say, there were more important things to spend the wages on.

Soap made with potash tends to be gelatinous—'soft soap' is potash soap—and also rather irritant to the skin. Medieval soap would still contain the glycerine that is produced as a by-product (it is extracted now, and sold for making nitro-glycerin, paint, and other purposes), and, contrary to popular belief and advertisers' claims, glycerine is not good for the skin as it tends to extract the essential moisture. Harder and milder soap can be made by using soda as the alkali instead of potash, and both kinds of soap were made in the Middle East: in Europe, however, the only method known for making soda soap was to mix the ordinary potash soap with salt. The resulting compound must have been distressing to use, for salt prevents soap from dissolving in water or lathering.

Some householders tried to make their soap a little more pleasant by adding oil of almonds, musk, civet, and other perfumes, or more homely ingredients such as rose petals and lavender. Such perfume materials were in great demand, and were very necessary to cover up the overpowering smell of unwashed bodies and unwashed clothes. The poorer people only had the clothes they worked and slept in, with perhaps a suit of 'best' to be taken out on great occasions. The rich had more clothes, but tended to wear a great many of them at the same time: in any case, there seems to have been very little idea of washing clothes between wearings. Another dose of perfume was the usual remedy when the clothes became too unpleasant. (Henry VIII was rather more fastidious than most of his subjects, and had his shirts washed occasionally. As he paid one penny per shirt, which would have been about half a day's pay for the laundress, it was clearly an expensive luxury, suitable for the royal purse, but not to be indulged by lower orders.)

The favourite perfumes, musk, civet, castor, and ambergris, were well chosen to cover up the smell of unwashed bodies and soiled clothes. They are what the modern perfumer calls 'animal notes'—musk is extracted from a gland near the penis of the musk deer, which lives mainly in the Atlas and Himalayan mountains. Civet comes from a similar gland in the civet cat, found in Abyssinia. The soft, waxy, incredibly 'cat'-smelling material is taken from the gland with a spoon, and traditionally packed in horns to transport it. The yield can be increased by teasing the civet cat before taking the wax. Castor comes from a sexual gland of the Russian beaver. Ambergris is a wax with a 'sweet-decaying' odour produced during an intestinal disease of the sperm whale. When the whale dies and decomposes, the wax floats up to the surface of the sea: sometimes it is found by beachcombers, and at many pounds an ounce it is a better find than Spanish gold.

All these perfume materials have odours in which sweetness, rottenness, and sexual elements are combined. They are used in small proportions in nearly all good modern perfumes, to give a hint of primitive sexual attraction, but to modern tastes it would be unthinkable to use them undiluted. A modern woman wearing pure civet as perfume might hope to suggest the mysterious aura of femininity, but she would be more likely in fact to suggest a nasty accident with a pet tom-cat. Montaigne, on the subject of smells, reminds us of an earlier standard, dating from Roman times:

'That is why Plautus says: *Mulier tum bene olet ubi nihil olet,* a woman smells best when she does not smell at all. And there is reason to suspect those who use fine additional scents, and to conclude that the perfumes are used to conceal some natural defect in that respect.'

Many of the medieval courtiers must have smelled rather like tom-cats anyway, so civet on the gloves was reasonably appropriate. Gloves and handkerchiefs were the favourite places for wearing perfume—'I only need to touch my whiskers with my gloves or my handkerchief for the perfume to stick to them for the rest of the day,' says Montaigne in the same essay—and the trades of glover and perfumer became almost synonymous. Most of the perfumes came to Europe through the thriving trade of Arabian merchants, who could call upon civet from Abyssinia, castor from Russia, musk from India, spices from Ceylon, and even perfumes from China, with equal ease. Together with the aromatic gums from the Middle East itself— myrrh, gum benzoin, frankincense—all the best perfumery was carried out in the Arab countries, and all the finest materials came from there. '. . . all the perfumes of Arabia will not sweeten this little hand . . .' says Lady Macbeth, showing that Shakespeare still regarded perfumes as an essential part of the washing or decontamination process, not the additional refinements that they have become now. Lady Macbeth would not have used soap.

Some shipments came direct to England from farther afield: in Dekker's *Shoemaker's Holiday* the Dutch skipper, trying to dispose of the goods on his ship, lists the treasures he has brought from Candy (Ceylon):

'Ick sal yow wat seggen, Hans; dis skip, dat comen from Candy, is al vol, by Got's sacrament, van sugar, civet, almonds, cambrick, end alle dingen, towsand towsand ding . . .'

Civet was valuable—perhaps more valuable, in real terms of labour content, in Elizabethan times than it is today. Somewhere in Abyssinia a hunter stalked a civet cat, an animal as fierce as a Highland wild cat, trapped it, tied it down and spooned out the waxy civet, then released the angry animal to run away and produce more civet. The perfume would be packed in a zebu horn and carried by runner to one of the towns, thence sold to an Arabian merchant, and shunted around the Mediterranean at steadily increasing prices until it was bought by an English glover, full of tales of the fabulous riches of his English clients, and with a strong-arm man at his side to protect the precious merchandise.

The horn would be sailed across the Channel, taxed on a fairly arbitrary basis in one of the English ports, and find its way to London, to add its rank sweetness to the atmosphere of the Elizabethan court.

. . .'Pah, pah! Give me an ounce of civet, good apothecary, to sweeten my imagination,' says King Lear: it is better, however, not to try to imagine the exact smell of the unwashed medieval lady or gentleman, in layers of unwashed wool, drenched in concentrated essence of civet cat.

5. *Over the Nasty Sty*

'First, her bedchamber,
(Where I confess, I slept not; but profess
Had that was well worth watching,) it was hang'd
With tapestry of silk and silver; the story,
Proud Cleopatra, when she met her Roman . . .
. . . The chimney
Is south the chamber; and the chimney-piece
Chaste Dian, bathing: never saw I figures
So likely to report themselves . . .
. . . The roof o' the chamber
With golden cherubins is fretted: her andirons
(I had forgot them) were two winking Cupids
Of silver, each on one foot standing, nicely
Depending on their brands.'

Cymbeline, II, 4

The quality that impressed every visitor to England in the late Tudor period was the richness of decoration and furnishing in the great houses. With the civil war of Yorkists and Lancastrians behind them, the Elizabethans in particular began to think in terms of a truly domestic architecture—houses built to live in, and not necessarily made to withstand a siege. Housewives could turn their attention to linen, furniture, and hangings: in the troubled times of Edward IV Margaret Paston seemed to spend more time counting the crossbows and arbalests than counting the spoons.

The moat and drawbridge gave way to gardens and terraces,

the windows grew larger (the Pastons, in their voluminous letters, showed a very wise preference for arrow slits—windows of the Elizabethan style would have been impossible to fortify or defend) and homely comforts became one of the legitimate aims of the house-builder:

'. . . For *Inbowed Windows* I hold them of good use; (in Cities indeed *Upright* do better, in respect of Uniformity towards the Street) for they be pretty Retiring Places for Conference; and besides, they keep both the Wind and the Sun off . . .'*

The great galleried halls, intended for dining, dancing, the display of treasures in cabinets, and the hanging of choice tapestries (in a word, for ostentation), were graced by staircases, a new type of ornament to the house. With their shallow risers, generous landings, carved balusters and newel posts complete with heraldic animals, these staircases were an elaborate symbol of the house seen as a *machine à habiter*, not as a defensive shell, and the bedchambers completed this effect. Not many bed-chambers could be as richly furnished as Imogen's regal apartment, but the Elizabethans did their best to follow the sumptuous lead of their sovereign and her greater nobles. The rooms, which still look rich and splendid today, must have been brighter and more brilliant when the tapestries were unfaded, the oak wainscots and panels were light, or painted, and the pictures not darkened by four centuries of oxidation in the varnish. Imogen was given tapestries of 'silk and silver' by Shakespeare (the '*Enchanted Palaces* of the *Poets*, who build them with small Cost', remarks Bacon acidly) but the living Queen had her dining-hall in Whitehall hung with tapestries of gold, sat on gold-embroidered cushions at Nonsuch, and under gold-painted ceilings in almost every great house.

The great trouble came with the floor. Erasmus, a great theologian, a good friend of England, and companion spirit to Sir Thomas More, wrote in disgust to Cardinal Wolsey's physician: 'The floors are made of clay, and covered with marsh rushes, constantly piled on one another, so that the bottom layer remains sometimes for twenty years incubating spittle, vomit, the urine of dogs and men, the dregs of beer, the remains of fish, and other nameless filth. From this an exhalation rises to the heavens, which seems to me most unhealthy. . . .'

*Bacon, *Of Building*.

Sir John Davies in *Epigrammes*, 1590, confirms that conditions were no better sixty years after Erasmus's complaint: he speaks of a country house hall as 'stinking with dogs and muted all with hawks'—perhaps the same rushes were in use. Some houses had supplies of rushes every month, but many made the same ones do, and just spread a few clean ones over the collection of 'rushes plus' described by Erasmus. With rats, mice, fly maggots, fleas, and all the other small creatures attracted by waste food, the floors must have been rather populous, and these inhabitants would have spread to any warm hiding-place that offered.

The fashions of the time, especially in the earlier part of the sixteenth century, gave them plenty of warm hiding-places. Padding was almost universal in any clothes that aspired to be fashionable: men wore the great padded breeches, stuffed with hair and flock, padded doublets (the 'peascod-bellied' doublet which came in around 1575 had enough stuffing to suggest pregnancy), padded rolls around the armholes of the doublet so as to give a manly shoulder line, and additional layers of linen in winter. In Minsheu's *Pleasant and Delightful Dialogues* the servants checking their master's laundry note that he has worn 'two pairs of linen breeches next the skin and three pair of linen hose under the stockings'.

Women wore hooped skirts with a bell- or coned-shaped framework at the waist, the farthingale, several petticoats, sometimes a thick padded roll around the waist (for the 'French' style), padded stomachers, padding on the arms and shoulders similar to that worn by men, and again several pairs of stockings or socks in cold weather. Such clothes would have been a paradise for fleas and lice.

Later in the century, some of the padding was taken out of breeches, but necessity applied it to the furniture: '. . . wainscot stools so hard that, since great breeches were laid aside, men can scant endure to sit on,' according to Sir John Harington. The simple wooden furniture of the early Tudor period became upholstered—'six high stools of walnut-tree covered with black velvet quilted' occurs in the Kenilworth inventory of 1583, and is typical of the conversion period.

Padding was added to the most unexpected pieces of furniture. A close stool made in 1547 for the 'use of the kynges mageste' was covered in black velvet and garnished with ribbons, fringes, and quilting involving the use of 2,000 gilt nails, thus allowing Edward VI to relieve himself in comfort. This commode was made like a box with a lid, and had two leather cases to carry the actual pot and a 'sesstorne' or cistern of water for washing it out—a rudimentary water-closet. A similar piece of furniture, used by Elizabeth I and later by James I, is still in existence at Hampton Court. It is covered with crimson velvet over thick upholstery, and has a lock for the lid, so that no one of lower order than the sovereign could use it —and also probably so that no one could tamper with it. James in particular was terrified of poisoning, and might have thought that poison in his close-stool would be a peculiarly nasty kind of death in the pot. No one seems to have used the piece of furniture after James I, which is not entirely surprising.

Those people who were not eligible for the padded seats of the mighty had to make do with the ordinary privy, or *jakes*. They might have had the advantages of a cleaner lavatory had anyone taken notice of another piece of Sir John Harington's writing, *The Metamorphosis of Ajax: A Cloacinean Satire*, in which Sir John describes a valve water-closet, invented by him and built for him at Kelston, near Bath. It was indeed a metamorphosis for the jakes as known to his contemporaries.

AN ANATOMY

In the privy that annoys you, first cause a cistern, containing a barrel, or upward, to be placed either in the room or above it, from whence the water may, by a small pipe of lead of an inch be conveyed under the seat in the hinder part thereof (but quite out of sight); to which pipe you must have a cock or a washer, to yield water with some pretty strength when you would let it in.

Next make a vessel of an oval form, as broad at the bottom as at the top; two feet deep, one foot broad, sixteen inches long; place this very close to your seat, like the pot of a close-stool; let the oval incline to the right hand.

This vessel may be brick, stone or lead; but whatsoever it is, it should have a current of three inches to the back part of it (where a sluice of brass must stand); the bottom and sides all smooth, and dressed with pitch, rosin, and wax; which will keep it from tainting with the urine.

In the lowest part of the vessel which will be on the right hand, you must fasten the sluice or washer of brass, with solder or cement; the concavity, or hollow thereof, must be two inches and a half.

To the washers stopple must be a stem of iron as big as a curtain rod; strong and even, and perpendicular, with a strong screw at the top of it; to which you must have a hollow key with a worm to fit that screw.

This screw must, when the sluice is down, appear through the plank not above a straw's breadth on the right hand; and being duly placed, it will stand about three or four inches wide of the midst of the back or your seat.

Item, That children and busy folk disorder it not, or open the sluice with putting in their hands without a key, you should have a little button or scallop shell, to bind it down with a vice pin, so as without the key it will not be opened.

These things thus placed, all about your vessel and elsewhere, must be passing close plastered with good lime and hair, that no air come up from the vault, but only at your sluice, which stands close stopped; and it must be left, after it is voided, half a foot deep in clean water.

If water be plenty, the oftener it is used, and opened, the sweeter; but if it be scant, once a day is enough, for a need, though twenty persons should use it.

If the water will not run to your cistern, you may with a force of twenty shillings, and a pipe of eighteen pence the yard, force it from the lowest part of your house to the highest.

Harington's closet, therefore, contains all the features of the modern lavatory—water to flush the bowl, delivered with enough force to clear it, and led in through a point near the rim of the bowl so as to wash it down completely, and a reservoir of water always in the bowl. This ensured, and ensures now, that the surface is never directly contaminated, and also acts as a trap against foul air coming up from the sewer. The only invention of note that Sir John did not foresee was the addition of the U-trap to maintain the reservoir automatically: he employed a valve operated by the user.

It is a sad reflection on the power of names that Harington's

'Satire' was not recognized as the eminently reasonable and civilized treatise that it is. Lytton Strachey, in *Elizabeth and Essex* refers to Harington as the writer of 'a Rabelaisian satire on water-closets', as if the *Metamorphosis of Ajax* were merely some scatological squib: it seems doubtful whether Strachey ever read the work, or whether, indeed, he realized that water-closets had not existed at the time. Other writers have followed suit in treating Harington as a joker with a public-school sense of humour.

In his own time he received little more attention. Apart from the great original at Kelston, only one other 'Harington' seems to have been built, at the Palace at Richmond. The original passed out of use very soon after Harington's death in 1612—perhaps no one else could unravel the secret of the 'little button or scallop shell' that protected the key of the valve from meddling fingers—but it failed mainly because it was isolated from the technology of its time. A water-closet, valuable though it is in itself, needs not only a mechanism such as the one that Harington designed, but also a ready supply of water and a sewer to take the foul water away—matters that he left to the builder of the closet. The water might be provided by a spring or small stream, if you were lucky enough to have such ready supplies of water on your extensive lands, but for most households water had to be carried on the shoulders of women from rivers and wells, and it was trouble enough to provide the water for cooking and laundering, without bringing more for luxuries such as water-closets.

Drainage was even more difficult. Landowners with riparian rights could run their closets into the river (and be damned to the other fellows downstream!) and no doubt Queen Elizabeth did so at Richmond, as the palace grounds run down to the Thames, but other users would have had to lay a sewer, and such a co-operative exercise was beyond the comprehension of the day. We admire the fierce individuality that drove Sir Francis Drake, that genial pirate, around the world, and English merchants into every foreign port; that achieved, at times, a grudging religious tolerance for the dissenters; we think of Sir Walter Raleigh, betrayed by his friends and his king, taking a last pipe of tobacco on the scaffold. The same individuality produced monopolies, so that even the necessities of life were taxed to enrich a few greedy royal favourites, and made collective action, whether for roads, water supply, or sewers, seem un-English. Until such action became possible, the water-closet had to remain an isolated eccentricity of an intelligent rich man, like the imaginary closets of Sir Ferdinando Lapith, in Aldous Huxley's *Crome Yellow*. Huxley's invention, obviously based on Sir John Harington, believed that 'the necessities of nature are so base and brutish that in obeying them we are apt to forget that we are the noblest creatures of the universe'. To counteract these degrading effects, he decided that privies must be placed as near to heaven as possible, and therefore constructed his house with immense towers dedicated to this purpose, with tremendous shafts separating the noblest creature of the universe from his earthly detritus.

Harington had other eccentricities besides his dislike of the unwashed privy. He urged a daily bath—'love you to be cleane and well apparelled, for from our cradles let us abhor uncleanliness, which neither nature nor reason can endure . . .' and indulged in bathing himself, much to the amusement of his contemporaries. He had some support from his godmother, Queen Elizabeth, who not only had the water-closet constructed at Richmond, but commanded the installation of baths at Windsor Castle, taking a bath once a month, we are told, 'whether she need it or no'. But for the mass of her subjects, this was a luxury they were quite prepared to forgo, and so was Harington's curious invention.

Even in courts and court circles, simpler customs were in vogue. One of the light-hearted stories of Pierre de Bourdeille, Seigneur and Abbé de Brantôme, concerns Francis I of France, that earlier 'Sun-King'. The king visited one of his favourite court ladies when, unfortunately, she was entertaining another lover. In the best tradition, she hid the gallant behind a pile of green branches lying in the hearth.

> When the king had performed his duties with the lady, he wanted to make water, and got out of bed. Finding no other place near at hand, he went to the hearth, and watered the poor lover just like a garden watering-can, from all sides, on his face, in his eyes, his nose, his mouth, everywhere; some even went down his throat. I leave you to imagine how the

knight felt, because he did not dare move, and what patience and endurance he displayed! When he had finished, the king bade the lady good-bye, and left. She locked the door behind him and called the gallant into her bed to warm him, and had him put on a clean shirt, and all not without laughter, after their great alarm. . . .

A clean shirt, one notes, but no mention of washing. The curious beliefs that equate filth with manliness or worth, 'honest dirt', and so on, were already well-established. In Nashe's *The Unfortunate Traveller* he puts forward the traditional soldier's view:

A company of coystrell Clearkes . . . outfaced the greatest and most magnanimious Servitors in their sincere and fini-graphicall cleane shirts and cuffs. A Lowce (that was anie Gentleman's companion) they thought scorne of, their nere-bitten beards must in a devill's name be dewed everye day with Rose-water, Hogges could have nere a haire on their backs for making them rubbing-brushes to rouse their Crab-lice. They would in no wise permit that the moates in the Sunbeames should be full mouthd beholders of their cleane phinified apparel, their shooes shined as bright as a slike-stone, their hands troubled and soyled more water with wash-ing, than the Cammell doth, that never drinks till the whole streame be troubled. Summarily, never anie were so fantas-ticall the one halfe as they.

The 'gentleman's companion' clung closely to those manly fellows who could not be troubled with rubbing-brushes and other louse-disturbers. Lice like a quiet life, grazing peacefully on the blood of their hosts, holding on to the body hairs with the highly efficient claws at the ends of their six legs—the claws of the crab-louse are large enough to be seen with the naked eye, hence the name. Those that infest man are of three types, each keeping to its natural boundaries as carefully as trade unionists in a demarcation dispute. The head louse, *Pediculus capitis*, clings to the hair on the head, and lays its eggs in small horny cells, *nits*, which are so firmly stuck to the hair that only methy-lated spirit will remove them (hairdressers have, or used to have, a special concoction made with soft soap and spirit which was swiftly brought out when a customer appeared with the characteristic lumps attached to the hair). The body louse, *Pediculus corporis*, ranges over the rest of the body but is rarely seen above the ears; even so it likes hair to cling on to, and chooses the legs, arms, underarms, and the masculine chest for most of its activity. The crab louse, *Phthirus pubis*, is a smaller creature that confines its attentions to pubic hair, and is the most resistant to removal, owing to the number of places that it can find in which to hide.

All of them creep quietly about from place to place on the body, without the vulgar ostentation of the flea, and all of them suck blood. Very often the bites themselves are not noticed, only the irritation set up by infection, so that the host to the lice is always scratching a little too late to disturb the creatures themselves. Unfortunately, although lice do not usually infect bites by regurgitating infected blood, they are careless about other points of hygiene, and deposit infected excrement near bites. Scratching opens up the bites and disease germs from the near-by excrement are rubbed into the wound. It is this insidious attack which is so repulsive about lice. One can sympathize with Thomas Moufet (reputed father of the better-known Miss Muffet, unwilling entomologist) who wrote in praise of fleas: 'Though they trouble us much, yet they neither stink as Wall lice doe, not is it any disgrace to a man to be troubled with them, as it is to be lowsie.' 'Wall lice' are obviously bugs, but it is interesting to note that even in Elizabeth's reign there was some distinction between lice and fleas as a criterion of hygiene.

The main disease carried by lice is typhus, known variously as 'jail fever', 'trench fever', pestilential fever, putrid fever, Brill's disease, and hospital fever: most of the names suggest its association with crowded conditions or its demoralizing effects. First the temperature rises, the teeth and tongue become coated, there is a feeling of intense thirst. Then an eruption appears on the body and spreading to the face: dark red blotches or spots. This is the most merciful stage of the disease, as the patients become torpid and stupid, succumbing to the 'typhous stupor', with delirium, and they lie with their eyes wide-open muttering, but unconscious of anything going on around them. For typhus victims in the trenches, or in an early hospital. this stage must have been a happy release from reality. Some, but not many, recovered from the stupor: for most it deepened into eternal sleep. Contemporary treatment, in Elizabethan times, was to administer opium, which no doubt eased the discomfort of the last hours, but cannot have produced any startling cures. Lice, and the typhus they carried with them from soldier to soldier, must have done more than any of the warring factions to make England, as Shakespeare said of Henry VI, 'his realm a slaughter-house, his subjects slain', and the little creatures contributed greatly to the losses on both sides of the Channel in the long-drawn-out struggle for France. However, they lacked Shakespeare to immortalize them.

Another scourge spread by lice, and perhaps also by ticks, was the sweating sickness that swept through the nation, and particularly the armies, in 1485, 1507, 1517, 1528, and 1551. It travelled through northern and eastern Europe, reached London in 1528 (causing Henry VIII to retire hastily to Hampton Court and then to various other centres, avoiding the sickness rather as a man avoids a persistent wasp).

John Caius, the eminent physician, has left a memoir of the last great outbreak in 1551: the disease began with a sense of foreboding, then cold shivers, giddiness, headache, and severe pains in the neck. These shivers lasted an hour or two only before they were suddenly overtaken by heat and violent sweating, delirium, and collapse. Many sufferers died in as little as three hours from the first chill.

Nashe describes the disease as seen through the eyes of the English soldiers:

> This sweating sickness, was a disease that a man then might catch and never goe to a hot-house. Manie Masters desire to have such servants as would worke till they sweate again, but in those dayes hee that sweate never wrought againe. That Scripture then was not thought so necessarie, which sayes, Earne thy living with the sweat of thy browes, for then they earnd their dying with the sweat of their browes. It was inough if a fat man did but trusse his points, to turne him over the pearch: Mother *Cornelius* tub why it was like hell, he that came into it, never came out of it.
>
> Cookes that stand continually basting their faces before the

fire, were now all cashierd with this sweat into kitchin stuff: their hall fell into the Kings hands for want of one of the trade to uphold it.

Felt makers and Furriers, what the one with the hot steame of their wooll new taken out of the pan, and the other with the contagious heat of their slaughter budge and conie-skinnes, died more thick than of the pestelence: I have seen an old woman at that season having three chins, wipe them all away one after another, as they melted to water, and left hir selfe nothing of a mouth but an upper chap. Looke how in May or the heat of Summer we lay butter in water for feare it should melt away, so then were men faine to wet their clothes in water as Diers doo, and hide themselves in welles from the heat of the Sunne.

Then happie was he that was an asse, for nothing will kill an asse but colde, and none dide but with extreme heate. The fishes called Sea-Starres, that burne one another by excessive heate, were not so contagious as one man that had the Sweate was to another . . .

From the descriptions left by Caius and Nashe, the sweating sickness seems to have been a particularly violent form of relapsing fever. Relapsing fever strikes communities in all parts of the world, causing exactly the symptoms of chills, followed by violent sweating and delirium, as in Caius's description of 'the Sweate'. It is still common in Africa, but has occurred in almost every country. An outbreak in Ireland in 1826 enabled doctors to distinguish it from typhus and typhoid fevers, and in 1873 Obermeier discovered the relapsing fever germ, *Spirillum obermeieri*, which is carried by lice and some forms of tick, especially *Ornithodoros moubata*. Lice and ticks are both attracted by warmth and moisture, so there is probably a great deal of truth in Nashe's embroideries about cooks and felt makers, and Caius's comment that the disease seemed to strike the well-clothed rich even more than the ragged poor. Ticks spread from animals to man quite easily (children still occasionally pick them up in the summer months) and are particularly adept at infecting their hosts, as their sucking probe is barbed, like a bee's sting, and tends to remain in the skin if the body of the tick is pulled off. The irritation caused by this foreign body in the skin sets up inflammation, and the warmth of the inflammation incubates the *Spirilla* germs.

Across the Channel, the French called sweating sickness the 'English Sweat', and ascribed it to the foggy climate of the country: Caius blamed it squarely on the filthy habits of the English, and confirms the opinions of Erasmus.

> Rich men, trust not in wealth,
> Gold cannot buy you health;
> Physic himself must fade;
> All things to end are made;
> The plague full swift goes by;
> I am sick, I must die—
> > *Lord, have mercy on us!*
> Beauty is but a flower
> Which wrinkles will devour;
> Brightness falls from the air;
> Queens have died young and fair;
> Dust hath closed Helen's eye;
> I am sick, I must die—
> > *Lord, have mercy on us!*

says Nashe (*In Time of Pestilence*), summing up in lapidary phrases the shortness of Elizabethan life. Plague, typhus, the sweat, all lent an added urgency to the feeling of 'so much to do, so little time'. Shakespeare's

> Golden lads, and girles all must,
> As Chimney-Sweepers come to dust

implies not only the inevitability of death, but its presence at every elbow.

6. *Sweete Themmes Run Softly*

Yet Nashe could put aside his fears of death, and forget his professional journalist's interest in picturesque horrors, to produce songs of limpid joy:

> Spring, the sweet spring, is the year's pleasant king;
> Then blooms each thing, then maids dance in a ring,
> Cold doth not sting, the pretty birds do sing—
> Cuckoo, jug-jug, pu-we, to-witta-woo!

Elizabeth's poets, when they turned to song, seemed to live in a perpetual springtime. Perhaps the promise of spring was closer to them. England was still mostly countryside—outside of London, Norwich, Bristol, and a handful of other towns, village life was the only way of life, and Londoners were still within walking distance of the open fields. London had a population around 75,000 in 1500, growing to 200,000 in 1600, or about the present populations of Worthing and Plymouth, respectively, but the country held about eight million sheep: even the metropolitan Nashe could write

> The palm and may make country houses gay,
> Lambs frisk and play, and shepherds pipe all day . . .

without any affectation of a 'pastoral mood', because such country sights were within a half-hour walk from the city. Spring meant relief from the long dark hours of winter, from salted meat and musty grain, relief from the constant anxiety that the harvest of last year might not last until the next. After the long struggles between Yorkist and Lancastrian, with the inevitable spoilage and neglect of the land that such a war entails, the Elizabethans were building up their fortunes again, and each spring must have seemed a new opportunity to enjoy life more fully. The poets echoed this atavistic joy in the rebirth of the year—Nashe, Peele, Campion, Sidney, Shakespeare, Fletcher, Dowland—England's song writers seemed to break into melody all together, like a dawn chorus of birds.

> Whenas the rye reach to the chin,
> And chopcherry, chopcherry ripe within,
> Strawberries swimming in the cream,
> And schoolboys playing in the stream;

Peele lists the pleasures of the spring with artless felicity.

But the schoolboys playing in the stream might have thought twice, had it not been for the intoxication of the spring sunlight. Although the streams were not contaminated, as they are today, with chemical residues, they were the drains for the greater part of the population. Fish found this kind of contamination no bother, and Henry VIII's polar bear, which he kept in the menagerie in the Tower, used to be allowed out on the end of a long chain to catch its own salmon in the Thames. Indeed, salmon flourished in the Thames up to the nineteenth century: in 1746 a water-bailiff could write proudly 'though some of our Northern Counties have as fat and as large (salmon) as the River *Thames*, yet none are of so exquisite taste . . .'

However, fish are not fussy about ordure: it was chemical contamination that drove salmon out of most of our rivers. They can thrive on organic material, however unpleasant it may seem to us, as many people have found to their cost after eating shellfish plumped up in areas where untreated sewage is discharged into the sea.

In 1539 the Fleet Ditch was covered in by order of the Court of Aldermen, during a series of works leading to the building of the Old Bailey, and this already noisome stream became a dark, stinking tunnel, the forerunner of underground sewers. Plain-spoken Ben Jonson took the Fleet Ditch for his subject in a mock-heroic poem 'On the Famous Voyage' (*Epigramme* 133), imagining a pair of travellers after a convivial evening at the Mermaid Tavern taking a wherry to Holborn. This involved a journey from Bread Street, where the Mermaid was situated, to Bridewell Dock on the Thamesside, and thence up the Fleet (along the route where, now, the Farringdon Road passes under the Holborn Viaduct). The dock itself is described first, and gives a more accurate view of the Thames than 'schoolboys playing in the stream':

> ... Say, thou stop thy nose:
> 'Tis but light pains; Indeed this Dock's no rose.
> In the first jawes appear'd that ugly monster,
> Ycleped Mud, which, when their oares did once stirre,
> Belch'd forth an ayre, as hot, as at a muster
> Of all your night-tubs, when the carts doe cluster,
> Who shall discharge first his merd-urinous load:
> Thorough her wombe they make their famous road,
> Between two walls; where, on one side, to scar men,
> Were seene your ugly Centaurs, yee call Car-men,
> Gorgonian scolds, and Harpyes: on the other
> Hung stench, diseases, and old filth, their mother ...

After this elegant comparison between the Thames mud and the contents of the night-soil carts, the wherry passes into the covered Fleet Ditch, and has a narrow escape from collision with a barge carrying manure out to the fields beyond London. A load of manure is a powerful argument for asserting one's right of way.

Then danger threatens from above: the many privies which were directed straight down into the Fleet from the houses above:

> ... What croaking sound
> Is this we heare? of frogs? No, guts wind-bound,
> Over your heads: Well, row. At this a loud
> Crack did reporte it selfe, as if a cloud
> Had burst with storme, and downe fell, *ab excelsis*,
> Poore Mercury, crying out on Paracelsus ...

(a reference to the common use of mercury and its compounds

as laxatives: mercurous chloride, calomel, was in use for such purposes until relatively recently).

The other uses of the Fleet also appear:

> The sinkes ran grease, and haire of meazled hogs,
> The heads, houghs, entrailes, and the hides of dogs:
> For, to say truth, what scullion is so nastie,
> To put the skins, and offall in a pastie?
> Cats there lay divers had been flead and rosted,
> And after moldie growne, againe were tosted,
> Then, selling not, a dish was tane to mince 'hem,
> But still, it seemed the ranknesse did convince 'hem,
> For, here they were throwne in with the melted pewter,
> Yet drown'd they not. They had five lives in future . . .

Spring, the sweet spring, had disadvantages:

> . . . How dare
> Your daintie nostrills (in so hot a season,
> When every clerke eats artichokes, and peason,
> Laxative lettuce, and such windie meate)
> Tempt such a passage? when each privies seat
> Is fill'd with buttock? And the walles doe sweate
> Urine, and plaisters? when the noise doth beate
> Upon your eares, of discords so un-sweet?
> And out-cryes of the damned in the Fleet?
> Cannot the Plague-bill keepe you backe, nor bells,
> Of loud Sepulchres with their hourely knells,
> But you will visit grisly Pluto's hall . . .?

One of the great difficulties with all rivers, but particularly the Thames, was the degree to which the water was impeded by bridges, weirs, locks, and other works. These made the flow sluggish, and consequently any discharged sewage tended to deposit in evil-smelling piles. Even in early times, there had been complaints, statutes, and general grumbling about such hazards, not so much because of the health risks that they involved, but because of the restriction of navigation on the river. In 1197, for instance, Richard I (for a consideration of 1,500 marks, probably about £100,000 in today's money) vested the care of the river Thames in the hands of the Mayor and corporation of London, and removed the privileges of the keeper of the Tower of London in respect of river tolls:

Know ye all that we, for the health of our soul, our father's soul, and all our ancestor's souls, and also for the common weal of our City of London, and of all our realm, have granted and steadfastly commanded that all weirs that are in the Thames be removed, wheresoever they shall be in the Thames: also we have quitclaimed all that which the Keeper of our Tower of London was wont yearly to receive of the said eirs. Wherefore we will and steadfastly command, that no keeper of the said Tower, at any time hereafter, shall exact anything of anyone, neither molest nor burden, nor any demand make of any person by reason of the said weirs. For it is manifest to us . . . that great detriment and inconvenience hath grown to our said City of London, and also to the whole realm, by occasion of the said weirs . . .

Obviously Richard's will and steadfast command had little effect: the offending weirs persisted so well that they figure in Magna Carta in 1215: '. . . all weirs from henceforth shall be utterly put down by Thames and Medway, and through all England, except only by the sea coasts.' The actual Latin of the charter calls the obstructions *kidelli*, which are fish-traps, or kittles, the original pretty kettles of fish. Other obstructions were dams, built by mill-owners to improve the movements of their water-wheels, and channels or courses (*gorces*) for catching the rising salmon and trout, so that in a petition of the thirteenth century:

'The merchants who frequent the water between London and Oxford are disturbed by gortz, lokes, mills and many other nuisances; that William de Bereford and the rest have been so concerned *en švice du dit nostre Seignour le Roy* that they could not give the matter proper attention.'

The merchants continued to be disturbed: in 1348:

'Whereas the four great rivers, Thames, Severn, Ouse, and Trente, from ancient time have been open for the passage of ships and boats, for the common profit of the people, of late . . . there are so many and so great obstructions . . . building of wears and mills and fixing of piles and palings athwart the rivers by every lord against his own estate that ships can pass to London and other good towns of the realm only in times of extreme abundance of water (*outrageous cretin de ewe*).' There

were also complaints about the nuisance caused by throwing
rubbish, floor rushes, and sewage, into the rivers, but again the
number and repetition of the complaints suggests that the law
was held in light regard. In 1535 Act 27 of Henry VIII pro-
hibits the casting of such rubbish into the Thames: 'evilly
disposed persons have habitually cast in dung and filth, and
carried away shore piles and other timberwork, by reason
thereof, great shelfs and risings have of late growne in the farway
of the said river,' but little was actually done: in a later Act
there is an indication of the reluctance to act against male-
factors with any decisiveness, as the Privy Council 'thought not
convenient suddenlie to geve absolute sentence, for that in time
there might percase arise some other just matter for the more
full mayntenance of either of their claymes: and that alsoo the
citie not having at first the full of their demaunde would be the
more readie to reforme th'abuses in places limited unto them
whereby to deserve enlargement of ther graunts ...' or, in
other words, the Privy Council might make regulations, but
did not feel capable of enforcing them. Old London Bridge,
with its many small arches, added its own degree of obstruction
to the general slowness of the river: the Thames must have been
almost stagnant in many places, despite the tides, and because
of this slow movement the water was more easily affected by
frost.

'In (Queen Elizabeth's) seventh year (1565) on the one and
twentieth of *December* began a Frost, so extreme, that on *New-
Yeers* Even people passed over the Thames on foot; some played
at Foot-ball, some shot at pricks, as if it had been firm ground.
Yet this great Frost, the third of *January* at night began to thaw,
and by the fifth day, there was no Ice at all to be seen; which
sudden thaw caused great Inundations.'*

As an obstruction, this was at least more pleasant than an
occurrence on the Severn, also in Elizabeth's time:

'... on the four and twentieth of *February*, being a great
Frost, after a Flood which was not great, there came down the
river of *Severn* such a swarm of Flyes and Beetles, that they were
judged to be above a hundred Quarters; the Mills thereabout
were dammed up with them for the space of four dayes, and
were then cleansed by digging them out with Shovells.'

* Baker, *Chronicle.*

The 'locks' that caused so much trouble were, of course, not the complicated structures that now exist on our larger rivers, but simple movable dams, usually wooden gates operated by ropes. Most of the time these locks held the water at a convenient level to operate water-wheels: when a boat wished to pass the lock gate was opened and the boatman did his best to dodge the cascade of water, making use of ropes or cables to hold his boat stable. Obviously such gates, opened only at the convenience of the miller, were not only a cause of delays, but a hazard to craft. Strype, in his additional notes to Stow's *Survey of London*, records the efforts of a courageous campaigner against these obstructions:

> Whereof one *John Bishop* made a complaint to the Lord Treasurer *Burleigh*. To whom he shewed, how by these Stoppages of the Water, several Persons, to the Number of 15 or 16, in four Years only, had been drowned, and their Goods lost; having been Persons belonging to Barges and Vessels using the River. But notwithstanding these Complaints, about the Year 1584 or 1585, there were above Seventy locks and Wears (that is, Thirty more at least than there was but Six Years before.) And whereas before there were not above Ten or Twelve Barges employed to and fro, now the number was encreased to Fourscore; and were of much greater Bulk and Bigness than before was used. Some of these Locks were extraordinary dangerous in passing. The going up of the Locks were so steep, that every Year Cables had been broken that cost 400L, and Bargemen and Goods drowned. And in coming down, the Waters fell so high, that it sunk the Vessels, and destroyed corn and Malt wherewith they were laden.

As might have been expected, Burleigh did not reply, nor did the number of locks decrease. Not dismayed, Bishop addressed himself to the Queen herself, softening the message by putting it into verse. Of the forty-three quatrains, a few will suffice to give the gist of Bishop's petition (the little headlines beside each quatrain were presumably designed to put over the salient points in the not unlikely circumstance that the queen did not read all the 172 lines with the care they deserved):

The names	Mylls weares and locks men do them call
of the	that doe annoy that worthy streame
wrongs	Against the lawe they doe stand all
	but still the drownde those symple men.
A locke	One Farmer hath a Lock in store
of great	That hath made many a Child to weepe
Murther	Their mothers begg from dore to dore
(Marlow)	Their Fathers drowned in the deepe.
Swine and	Then being drowned they bury them there
dogges doe	where dogges and swyne then do them finde
eat mens	their fleshe they eat and all to teare
fleshe	which is contrarie to mankinde.

All considered the *Sweete Themmes* apostrophized by Spenser needed a great deal of poetic imagination to make it sweet in any way, and the other great rivers of the realm were in a similar deplorable condition. As the population increased, and the volume of their waste products became proportionately larger, the rivers became more contaminated. At the same time, the commercial interests of millers, farmers, and fishermen contrived to build more and more obstructions in the streams, so that the water-flow was often reduced almost to stagnation in times of drought.

As the rivers, so the roads. The city streets were still beaten mud, mixed with household slops that had been shot out from windows, and the country roads were only tracks. Stow describes the entry to London by Aldgate, along the road which is now Whitechapel High Street:

Also without the bars both sides of the street be pestered with cottages and alleys, even up to Whitechapel church, and almost half a mile beyond it, into the common field; all which ought to be open and free for all men. But this common field, I say, being sometime the beauty of this city on that part, is so encroached upon by building of filthy cottages, and with other purpressors, inclosures, and laystalls (notwithstanding all proclamations and acts of parliament made to the contrary), that in some places it scarce remaineth a sufficient highway for the meeting of carriages and droves of cattle; much less is there any fair, pleasant, or wholesome way for people to walk on foot; which is no small blemish to so famous a city to have so unsavoury and unseemly an entrance or passage thereunto.

We may, today, wonder whether the present Whitechapel High Street is any better advertisement for the entry to a great city, but it is at least fairly clean. London mud in the sixteenth and seventeenth centuries was so slimy and adhesive that nobody of 'quality' walked in the streets at all if they could possibly avoid it.

However, things must have been significantly worse in some other cities. Howell, a Londoner, wrote of the Paris streets in the early seventeenth century:

'This town is always dirty, and 'tis such a dirt, that by perpetual motion is beaten into such black unctuous oil that where it sticks no art can wash it off. . . . It also gives so strong a scent that it may be smelt many miles off if the wind be in one's face.'

Sometimes the mud was useful as a weapon. Unpopular characters ran the risk of a pelting if they appeared in the streets without adequate guard, and prisoners in the stocks or the pillory would be plastered unmercifully. A hard life and an oppressive social system do not engender delicacy or a sense of fair play in the mass of people, and the Elizabethan and Jacobean crowds were singularly lacking in either quality. They found only legitimate amusement in hurling mud, sticks, and stones at a helpless prisoner, often to the point where the victim sustained permanent wounds or even lost the use of an eye.

Mud-throwing could be symbolic. The Earl of Pembroke and other conspirators saw a chance to break the power of Robert Carr, Earl of Somerset, and James I's current boy-friend, by the fairly obvious step of introducing an even more attractive young man to the court, George Villiers, who after-wards became Duke of Buckingham. After a meeting in Bay-nard Castle during which it emerged that they had every chance of success in their plan, they rode back to London, and, passing down the crowded Strand, saw in a shop a portrait of Somerset on display: with an unerring instinct for the tawdry gesture they stopped and hurled handfuls of the street mud at the picture.

DIRT

> Such welcome and unwelcome things at once,
> 'Tis hard to reconcile.

James I journeyed down from Scotland overjoyed with the seemingly boundless riches of his new kingdom, and his court was the envy of all Europe. Damask, satin, velvet, cloth of gold and similar materials were everyday wear for the courtiers, to the extent that the added pearls and precious stones became the only means of displaying one's riches. The cities, bursting out from their walls into suburbs, market gardens, and warehouses, could furnish countless refinements of life, and the rich houses vied with one another in magnificent decoration and furnishing. The rivers provided fish in profusion, and also carried merchandise from all over the known world to supply the ever more complex demands of English life.

Yet, on the other hand, the damask and satin were dirty and sweat-stained, and the resources of Arabia could do little to conceal the rank smell of their wearers, the streets between the fine houses were mud-tracks littered with garbage, dung, and offal, and the rivers were open sewers. Political crisis was in the air, soon to explode into civil war, but another and more fundamental crisis was slowly building up in the quality of life itself.

7. *That Unspeakable Puddle of a Time*

Thus Carlyle, in his *Letters and Speeches of Oliver Cromwell*, vented his apparently limitless capacity for misanthropy on the whole of the Jacobean age. Like most of Carlyle's judgements, it is grossly unfair. From whatever angle we look at the seventeenth century, and whichever public scandals or abuses we select as evidence of its unpleasantness, there are parallels in other ages.

It was a time of political intrigue and unrest, it lurched into a civil war and religious strife: however, the civil war was less damaging than that outbreak of gang warfare called the Wars of the Roses, and the religious quarrels less bloody than those surrounding Mary and Elizabeth Tudor. It was a time of peculation and jobbing—but what period is not? It has a name for loose sexual morality, but for the mass of the people the pattern remained the same for an age before and after the Jacobean period—illegitimacy was rare but last-minute marriages almost the rule. It was a dirty age—among others just as dirty.

But one consideration lends point to Carlyle's disgust: King James himself. England has had weak kings, fond kings, and lazy kings in plenty; it has also had pompous and self-vaunting kings. Unfortunately, in James I and VI, the weakness and the belief in Divine Right of Kings were combined in grotesque concert. His extraordinary belief in his own superhuman powers only emphasized his sadly human shortcomings.

. . . his beard was very thin: his tongue too large for his mouth, and made him drink very uncomely, as if eating his drink, which came out into the cup of each side of his mouth; his skin was as soft as taffeta sarsnet, which felt so, because hee never washt his hands, onely rubb'd his fingers ends slightly with the wet end of a napkin; his legs were very weake, having had (as was thought) some foul play in his youth, or rather before he was born, that he was not able to stand at seven years of age, that weaknesse made him ever leaning on other mens shoulders; his walke was ever circular, his fingers ever in that walke fidling about his cod-piece . . .

Sir Anthony Weldon, who wrote his account of the king (published in 1650) for private circulation, was no friend of the Stuarts. He had been knighted by King James when he succeeded his father as Clerk of the Green Cloth, but dismissed after writing a scurrilous account of Scotland—by implication, an insult to the King of Scots himself. But on the other hand many of his strictures on James are repeated by other observers. One cannot expect criticism of the royal personage in public writings, but ambassadors sometimes send character assessments to their masters, and these are likely to be unbiased and also frank. M. de Fontenay, writing of James when he was still in Scotland, confirms some of Weldon's points:

'His manners, as a result of the failure to instruct him properly are aggressive and very uncivil, both in speaking, eating, clothes, games, and conversation in the company of women. He never stays still in one place, taking a singular pleasure in walking up and down, but his carriage is ungainly, his steps erratic and vagabond, even in his own chamber . . .'

Weldon goes on to note a habit that, combined with not washing and wearing heavily padded garments, must have made James unpleasant to approach:

'. . . In his dyet, apparrell and journeys, he was very constant; in his apparrell so constant, as by his good will he would never change his cloathes untill worn out to very ragges.'

He combined this graceless outward appearance with other, more fundamental weaknesses. He was the irritating type of homosexual who insists on promiscuous public embraces, directed to any attractive young man in his court. Fontenay says cautiously that one of his defects is 'That he loves indiscreetly and obstinately'; Sir Henry Wotton, writing a confidential dispatch for the Grand Duke of Tuscany, says 'He is very familiar with his domestics and gentlemen of the chamber'; but Francis Osborne, in his *Traditionall Memoyres* is more explicit, and also draws attention to another unpleasant effect of that 'tongue too large for the mouth':

'I have heard that Sir Henry Rich, since Earle of Holland, and some others, refused his majesties favour upon those conditions they subscribed to, who filled that place in his affection: Rich loosing that opportunity his curious face and complection afforded him, by turning aside and spitting after the king had slabered his mouth . . .'

James's boy-friends were wise enough not to show any such emotion. Weldon tells how James took his leave of Robert Carr in 1615:

'The earle, when he kissed his hand, the king hung about his neck, slabbering his cheeks, saying, "For Gods sake, when shall I see thee againe? On my soule, I shall neither eat nor sleep until you come again." The earle told him on Monday (this being on the Friday), "For Gods sake, let me," said the king— "Shall I, shall I?" then lolled about his neck. "Then, for Gods sake, give thy lady this kiss for me." In the same manner at the stayres head, at the middle of the stayres, and at the stayres foot.'

James often acted with the bitchy spitefulness characteristic of his particular type of homosexuality; afraid to assert himself over any major crimes or abuses, he would pursue small offenders with hysterical savagery, as when he ordered the Attorney General to issue a Star Chamber proclamation (a summons usually reserved for those guilty of murder or high treason) against a wretched poacher, Henry Field, who had taken a deer in the Royal Forest. (The proclamation was issued, State Papers 14–187, despite the Attorney General's carefully worded warning that such action would bring James into ridicule.) In his 'philosophical' discussions, the courtiers soon learned that no good would come of defeating the king in argument, and the more cunning ones would make deliberate mistakes in their debating points, so as to give him the pleasure of correcting them. Even his well-known tirades against tobacco may have been prompted by envy of Sir Walter Raleigh, whose memory and reputation obstinately survived the judicial assassination contrived by Count Gondomar, the Spanish ambassador.

James had a weak head for liquor, and though fond of 'frontiniack, canary, high country wine, tent wine, and Scottish ale', he did not drink much of them at a time: according to Weldon, 'he seldom drank at any one time above four spoonfulls, many times not above one or two'. His taste in food was equally Spartan, or Scottish: his favourite dish was reported as sheep's head, boiled with the wool on, and served with butter. The effects of a dish like this on the dribbling monarch, with his 'aggressive and uncivil' eating habits, and heavy quilted doublet perpetually slobbered with saliva, can be imagined, but are not to be dwelt on too long.

The weak head often failed him at convivial meetings, which were becoming increasingly common as the court subsided into excesses of all kinds:

'... in his old age, Buckingham's jovial suppers, when he had any turne to doe with him, made him sometimes overtaken, which he would the very next day remember and repent with tears.' (This quotation again comes from Weldon: it is a pity that Weldon never noticed the dangers of using 'he' too often in passages concerning two people, but we may take it that most of the 'he's' refer to James.)

Sometimes the Stuart court's partiality for wine operated not only on the King, but on guests and even performers called upon to entertain. Those of us who are only accustomed to the rather circumscribed orgies of the Royal Command Performance and similar affairs may compare these with an entertainment given at court for a visit of the Danish King Christian IV, a hard-drinking ruler who became a national hero at the unlikely age of sixty-seven. He visited England in July and August 1606, and Sir John Harington reported the proceedings to a friend with the same fastidious wit that illuminates his other writings:

Our feasts were magnificent, and the two royal guests did most lovingly embrace each other at table. I think the Dane hath strangely wrought on our good English nobles; for those, whom I never could get to taste good liquor, now follow the fashion, and wallow in beastly delights. The ladies abandon their sobriety and are seen to roll about in intoxication. In good sooth, the parliament did kindly provide his Majestie so seasonably with money, for there hath been no lack of good livinge; shews, sights, and banquetings, from morn to eve.

One day, a great feast was held, and after dinner, the representation of Solomon his Temple and the coming of the Queen of Sheba was made, or (as I may better say) was meant to have been made, before their Majesties, by device of the Earl of Salisbury and others. —But, alass! as all earthly thinges do fail to poor mortals in enjoyment, so did prove our presentment hereof. The Lady who did play the Queens part, did carry most precious gifts to both their Majesties; but, forgetting the steepes arising to the canopy, overset her caskets into his Danish Majesties lap, and fell at his feet, tho rather I think it was in his face. Much was the hurry and confusion; cloths and napkins were at hand, to make all clean. His Majesty then got up and woud dance with the Queen of Sheba; but he fell down and humbled himself before her, and was carried to an inner chamber and laid on a bed of state; which was not a little defiled with the presents of the Queen which had been bestowed on his garments; such as wine, cream, jelly, beverage, cakes, spices, and other good matters. The entertainment and show went forward, and most of the presenters went backward, or fell down; wine did so occupy their upper chambers. Now did appear, in rich dress, Hope, Faith, and Charity: Hope did assay to speak, but wine rendered her endeavours so feeble that she withdrew, and hoped the King would excuse her brevity: Faith was then all alone, for I am certain she was not joyned with good works, and left the court in a staggering condition: Charity came to the Kings feet, and seemed to cover the multitude of sins her sisters had committed ... She then return'd to Hope and Faith, who were both sick and spewing in the lower hall ... Now did Peace make entry, and strive to get foremoste to the King; but I grieve to tell how great wrath she did discover unto those of her attendants; and much contrary to her semblance, most rudely made war with her olive branch, and laid on the pates of those who did oppose her coming ...

Sometimes this gluttony had its aftermath. At a feast given by the Earl of Carlisle, an early favourite of the King's Scottish days, the board was piled high with the most costly dishes, made of such extravagant ingredients that, as Osborne says:

'I cannot forget one of the attendants of the king, that at a feast, made by this monster in excesse, eate to his single share a whole pye, reckoned to my lord at ten pounds, being composed of amber-grece, magisteriall of perle, musk, &c, yet was so far (as he told me) from being sweet in the morning, that he almost poysoned his whole family, flying himselfe like the satyr from his own stinck . . .'

Such excesses were not only the result of the increasing wealth of the country; they were the outward sign that authority, in any real sense, had passed out of the sovereign's hands. Extravagant feasts and masques could have been held in Elizabeth's day, and indeed great entertainments were given, when the occasion demanded it, but Elizabeth would never have allowed any of her subjects, however beloved or powerful, to waste her resources in useless ostentation. James did not care for feasts and shows for himself, but he could not bear to refuse anything to his lovers, and like spoiled children Carlisle, Somerset, Buckingham and the rest vied with one another to parade their easy-won riches. It is not surprising that the crowds shouted, 'God bless thee, little David!' as John Felton was taken to the Tower after murdering the Duke of Buckingham— Buckingham had become not only a Goliath, but a Moloch, devouring a monstrous share of the country's goods.

*

Away from the court, more thrifty means had to be used to keep up appearances. In the cities, one mark of riches was, curiously enough, the maintenance of wood fires, instead of 'seacole' fires. Cities had expanded, and the forests had contracted, until the cost of wood for fuel overtook that of coal. Henri Misson, a Huguenot refugee, has left a very detailed account of coal-burning in London—more detailed, possibly, than any English writer might have done, because the use of sea-coal was unknown in France at the time, and he set down every detail like an anthropologist describing a primitive rite— as perhaps our coal-fires seemed.

'Their common Fewel is Coal, which comes from Scotland and Newcastle ... they put into the Chimney certain Iron Stoves about half a foot high with a Plate of Iron behind and beneath; before and on each side are Bars placed and fasten'd like the Wiers of a Cage, all of Iron.'

After lighting the coal in the grate, another primitive rite was necessary:

'In proportion as the Coal grows hotter it dissolves, becomes glutinous, and sticks together ... to keep it up and Revive it you now and then give it a stir with a long piece of Iron, made on Purpose.'

The coal was softer than the house-coal of today, obtained by open-cast mining or from near the surface by 'bell-mining'. This meant digging a hole in the ground where the coal was fairly near the surface, and working downwards and outwards from the original pit until it became too difficult to raise the coal to the surface in baskets or tubs—or until the ground over the bell-shaped hole suddenly gave way, burying a few miners and making the pit uneconomic. Deep mining, with proper shafts and winding gear, did not come in until the nineteenth century.

The coal was brought from Newcastle and Scotland, partly because there were seams conveniently close to the surface, and partly because the roads were too bad for overland traffic, so coastal shipping was the only practicable means of transport. It was soft 'lignite' coal, half-way between peat and hard coal, and would tend to melt just as Misson describes, giving off at the same time incredible volumes of black smoke. As the chimneys in the Jacobean period were not usually very efficient, the effects on the houses were appalling: Misson adds cheerfully that the smoke is terribly thick, but 'one is soon used to it', and if the chimneys are well built it 'is carried cleanly away and consequently incommodes the Streets more than the Houses'. Complaints about the London atmosphere, in particular, grow more numerous and serious as the seventeenth century progressed (if that is the appropriate word), and the amount of coal landed in the port of London rose from 11,000 tons at the end of the sixteenth century to about 500,000 tons at the end of the seventeenth.

Not surprisingly, Misson notes that 'people of the first quality

burn wood in London' although even they could only afford it
for their bedchambers. In the country, wood was still the
standard fuel, supplemented by dried leaves, grass, and cow
dung in the south, and dried heather and peat in the north. As
coal-burning spread, it added to the already heavy soiling in
houses, and might have led to a greater demand for soap, had
not soap been so prohibitively expensive. In Naworth Castle
accounts for the early part of the century, soap of unspecified
quality was costing sixteen to nineteen shillings a firkin: this
would be about fourpence a pound in those times, or thirty
to forty new pence a pound in modern terms. Single soap balls
cost sixpence, about fifty new pence. Cleaning accessories were
also very expensive in real terms: a pail and dust basket, one
and six, or about £1·50, brooms sixpence to one shilling (fifty
new pence to £1), mops elevenpence, threepence to fourpence
a pound for starch (starching had been introduced in James's
reign, and enjoyed an immediate vogue for dressing the elaborate
ruffs which figure in portraits of the period). By contrast, a
year's wages for the maid who did the cleaning—when she did—
would be fifty to eighty new pence, or about the same number
of pounds now. Of course, she would have her keep, and in
a country house there would be little to spend the money on
except pedlar's fairings and similar little luxuries.

The washing processes that have survived in household
accounts and similar sources suggest that cleaning and laundering were major crises rather than everyday events. A stain
remover consisted of bull's gall, white of egg, burnt alum, salt,
orris powder, and soap, made into a ball and dried in a shady
spot until it was hard enough to rub over the clothes or linen
without falling to pieces. The rubbing, on the dampened cloth,
was followed by rinsing, and then, we are told, if the stain has
not gone, rub it again with the ball. And again and again,
presumably.

Pitch and candle-wax stains could be removed from clothes
and hats with a feather dipped in the finest oil of turpentine:
this would actually work, if slowly, and may still be recommended for our present-day scourge, oil and tar on beaches
which spreads on to clothes.

The sulphur in coal smoke blackens silver, and this must
account for the large number of curious recipes for silver

polishes which survive from the seventeenth century, especially as silver was becoming the favourite household decoration. Some recipes were simple, though not likely to be revived—urine and wood ashes were the main ingredients. Vine ashes were particularly prized, but the source of the urine seemed to have been a matter of indifference. Ashes of wheat straw, mixed with whiting and burnt alum, was another mixture, and a bath of 'Sal Armoniac', Sal Gem, Tartar, and Roman Vitriol was also recommended. This last formula is rather odd: sal ammoniac is ammonium chloride, and mixed with alkali it would give ammonia, which is still used in all good silver cleansers; 'Sal Gem' seems to have been a form of soda, which would act as the alkali. But Roman Vitriol is copper sulphate, which would do nothing to silver, but could be used to turn iron utensils to a coppery red. Indeed, there is a recipe for making iron look like gold which involves heating burnt alum, sal ammoniac, nitre, and strong vinegar in a brass pan, and then applying the liquid to the iron: the copper in this case would be dissolved away from the brass. Perhaps the housewife who laboriously copied down the 'silver cleaner' got things just a little wrong.

She would have had all her time occupied if she had followed the directions given by Mrs. Anne Blencowe, the daughter of John Wallis, the vainglorious mathematician, for whitening linen.

First soak the cloth from Saturday to Monday in a thick green mixture of soft water and sheep's dung (only summer dung will do). From Monday to Wednesday, dip the cloth repeatedly in a pond or river. On Wednesday beat out and leave to soak in a pond or river until Thursday afternoon, then allow to dry. Next day, put it in a tub, spread a buck sheet over it, make a thin paste of Dog's Mercury, Mallow, Kecks, or Wormwood, spread this over the buck sheet, then pour strong boiling lye over the sheet, cover and allow to stand overnight. By Friday it is ready to be spread on the grass and watered all morning. Friday night, repeat the whole process with Dog's Mercury, etc., and boiling lye, and again on Saturday. On Saturday night drop the cloth into a tub of lye and allow it to soak until Monday morning. It is then ready to be laid out once more and watered every day with pond water until white enough. ...

One's first reaction to this process is that it must, surely, be intended for some other purpose than whitening linen—preparing a compost heap, perhaps? The second reaction is to wonder exactly what part the dung and the various plants played in the process: Dog's Mercury (*Mercurialis perennis* Linn., adder's meat, boggart flower, boggart posy, dog flower, dog's medicine, green waves, snake's bit, snake's flower, snake's food, snake's meat, snake's victuals, or just simply snakeweed) is used in herbal medicine for enemas, but otherwise has all the characteristics that are summed up by the herbals: it is 'a hairy, creeping, foetid perennial', and it also tends to colour things yellow. Summer dung might act to some extent to remove bloodstains and similar deposits, but only at a cost to the general salubrity of the linen. And lastly, who actually did the work? Ten days of dabbling in sheep's dung and boiling lye, still extracted from wood ashes at this time, would leave little time or inclination for other household work.

Most of the contemporary recipes must have been difficult to follow except by enthusiasts. Alum was still brought from Germany at great expense (its main purpose was the tanning of fine leathers such as glove leather, a process known as tawing or whitawing to distinguish it from heavy leather tanning with tan bark, and a little was used, as now, as a styptic for cuts and sores). It was discovered in Yorkshire by Thomas Chaloner, who, according to Aubrey, 'tooke notice of the soyle and herbage, and tasted the water, and found it to be like that where he had seen the Allum workes in Germanie,' but not until the reign of Charles I. Sal ammoniac was brought from Arabia, where it was prepared from salt and camel's urine. Roman vitriol was still brought from Italy, as the name suggests, and tartar from the wine-growing districts of France, so all these homely recipes required considerable resources to prepare.

> Farewell, rewards and fairies,
> Good Housewives now may say,
> For now foul Sluts in dairies
> Do fare as well as they;

said Richard Corbet, Bishop of Norwich, about the decline in domestic manners and standards in the Jacobean age: Lady Anne Clifford, less publicly, confided to her diary that James's court in 1603 was a dirtier place than Elizabeth's court: '. . . we were all lousy by sitting in the chamber of *Sir Thomas Erskine*.'

It was in this environment of filth and neglect, oddly coupled with extravagance and artificiality in the court, that James's unfortunate second son grew up. He absorbed from his father and the crowd of flatterers round him the idea that the King was divine and untouchable, while all the time James's conduct and personal habits made it clear that the King was only too human—a dirty old man in both senses of the phrase. All kingly power is sustained by an illusion, the belief that there is something numinous about the King that gives him the right to control the lives of millions of people no less strong, wise, or deserving than himself. Henry VIII and his daughter Elizabeth possessed the numinous power without having to state it in words. James talked about the powers of a king continually, but his personal life gradually eroded any belief in them, sowing the seeds of doubt, the loss of illusions, that finally brought his son to a scaffold in Whitehall.

8. *Multitudes of Poor Pestiferous Creatures*

> Marke but this flea, and marke in this,
> How little that which thou deny'st me is;
> It suck'd me first, and now sucks thee,
> And in this flea our two bloods mingled bee;
> Thou know'st that this cannot be said
> A sinne, nor shame, nor losse of maidenhead,
> Yet this enjoyes before it wooe,
> And pamper'd swells with one blood made of two,
> And this, alas, is more than wee would doe.

John Donne, if not actually liking fleas, found them apt symbols for his elaborate metaphors and conceits. 'Women are like . . . Fleas sucking our very blood, who leave not our most retired places free from their familiarity, yet for all their fellowship will they never be tamed or commanded by us . . .'

John Gay, in *Man and the Flea*, suggests slyly that, just as man talks about the 'lower animals' because he sees them as created solely for his use or food, so might the flea claim to be superior to man. Man, according to this view, is merely a species of large cattle existing to feed fleas.

When they do feed, they carry out the operation as carefully as a milkmaid with a valuable animal. By instinct fleas seem to be able to choose places on the body that are difficult to scratch, yet offer plenty of escape routes, and once there they prepare the skin with care, scraping away with a stiletto-like proboscis until the skin is softened and any dead cell layers removed. Then, with an action rather like a swimmer diving from a springboard, the flea raises its tail in the air and drives its proboscis deep into the skin, to the point where small blood vessels occur. It injects saliva (estimated at about 0·004 cubic millimetres), which has anti-coagulating agents in it to stop the blood from clotting for several hours, and then sucks up the blood into its stomach, which slowly distends. When it is full, it lowers its abdomen, pulls out the proboscis, and usually excretes a certain amount of the half-digested blood on to the skin as a kind of libation. It will then usually retire to some sheltered hairy corner of the body to sleep. After a few hours the injected saliva begins to set up irritation, and the red mark on the skin becomes apparent, but by this time the flea is well away, and scratching only serves to rub germs into the bite.

Fleas had been carrying bubonic plague around Europe ever since the Black Death in 1348–9, and about the beginning of the seventeenth century the outbreaks grew more serious. In 1610–11 several towns and villages suffered epidemics as catastrophic as in the Black Death, and the disease spread more rapidly, so that one infected person could swiftly bring all his or her neighbours into danger. In Bottesford, Leicester, the burial of Katherine Havett in February 1609–10 (the year still ended on 25 March, so that February counted as nearly the end of 1609, not nearly the beginning of 1610) inspired the local vicar to doggerel verse:

> And here the Plague began, she dying poyson'd many,
> Th' infection was so great wher't came yt scarce left any.

There were 104 burials recorded in the parish register from February 1609–10 to December 1610, about six times as many as in a normal year for the small parish.

Sometimes plague was apparently associated with moral turpitude: an entry in the Great Coggeshall, Essex, parish register shows a regrettable lack of Christian charity:

1578 August 10 Lore Smith wife of John Smith was buried, the first to die of the Plague.

This Lore Smith was the instrument of the Lord used to bring the infection of the Plague into this town. She was the first that died of that infectious sickness and the most of those that followed dyed of the same, until the Winter time came, when the Lord in mercie stayed the same. The woeman was comanlie noted to be a notable harlot.

'These that followed' were of course further entries in the burials register, again greatly swelled by the plague victims.

In 1625, London was struck by a particularly sudden outbreak: John Evelyn, recalling this event in his childhood (he was five at the time) says:

'I was this year (being the first of the reign of King Charles) sent by my father to Lewes, in Sussex, to be with my grandfather, Standsfield, with whom I passed my childhood. This was the year in which the pestilence was so epidemical, that there died in London 5000 a-week, and I well remember the strict watches and examinations upon the ways as we passed; and I was shortly after so dangerously sick of a fever, that (as I have heard) the physicians despaired of me.'

The 'strict watches' were set up by every village and town to drive away any wanderers who might be suffering from the plague or carry the infection with them. As in the worst period of the Black Death, self-preservation came before humanitarianism or hospitality.

Defoe's *A Journal of the Plague Year* is a brilliant reconstruction, not an eye-witness report (it was published in 1722, fifty-seven years after the events of the Great Plague), but it gives the true flavour of the time.

> After this the parish officers came up to them and parleyed with them at a distance . . . John answered frankly that they were poor distressed people from London who, foreseeing the misery they should be reduced to if plague spread into the city, had fled out in time for their lives, and, having no acquaintance or relations to fly to, had first taken up at Islington; but, the plague being come to that town, were fled farther; and as they supposed that the people of Epping might have refused them coming into their town, they had pitched their tents thus in the open field and in the forest, being willing to bear all the hardships of such a disconsolate lodging rather than have any one think or be afraid that they should receive injury by them.
>
> At first the Epping people talked roughly to them, and told them they must remove; that this was no place for them;

and that they pretended to be sound and well, but that they might be infected with the plague for aught they knew, and might infect the whole country, and they could not suffer them there . . .

The 'history-book' events of the seventeenth century—the arrival of James I from Scotland, the Gunpowder Plot, Charles I and his parliaments, the Civil War, Great Rebellion or however we choose to call it, the Commonwealth, the Restoration, the deposition of James II, and so on—really affected only a tiny fraction of the population. Whether King or Parliament, Protestant or Catholic, were at the top of the heap, the lives of over four million of the five million Englishmen at the middle of the century were unchanged. They tilled the soil, lived hard, suffered chronic scurvy and rickets, respected their masters, bowed or curtseyed to the squire, and feared two things above all—a bad harvest and sickness. Both of these meant certain death. It is scarcely surprising that they viewed strangers with suspicion or downright enmity: strangers only brought trouble. It might be extra taxation (in which case their masters would bear down even harder on their workers to furnish the money), fighting, when the soldiers would occupy their houses, take their food, and seduce their daughters, without hope of recompense, or it might be city folk fleeing from plague, smallpox or typhus, and bringing the seeds of the disease with them. Often this enmity led to fighting: during the worst plague years gangs of Londoners would retire to the countryside in Essex and Kent, and if opposed would battle their way into villages for food and shelter.

Compared with this long-drawn-out and constant battle against disease, the Civil War seems no more than a ripple of trouble on an ocean of misery. The decisive battle of Naseby accounted for the deaths of 700 royalists and 200 parliamentary soldiers: every day of the 1625 and 1665 plagues saw the same number of sudden deaths. The New Model Army of 21,000 men could have been wiped out in one month's plague casualties for London alone.

The Great Plague of 1665 has become memorable for several reasons, although it was only one of a constant series of outbreaks which had continued for three hundred years. It was witnessed and reported by those two indefatigable diarists,

Samuel Pepys and John Evelyn, it was the subject of Defoe's masterly realistic novel, and it was also the last serious epidemic in this country—although plague continued to rage in Europe, and Vienna counts its 'Great Plague' as the outbreak of 1679. There had been no serious epidemic since the 1625 attack, and Londoners were almost able to forget the disease, especially as there were no written records of the 1625 plague apart from Bills of Mortality buried in dusty archives:

'We had no such thing as printed newspapers in those days to spread rumours and reports of things, and to improve them by the invention of men, as I have lived to see practised since. . .' says Defoe, with acid truth.

Occasional reports trickled through from the other side of the North Sea: in his record for 19 October 1663, Pepys notes: '. . . to the Coffee House in Cornhill; where much talk about the Turk's proceedings, and that the plague is got to Amsterdam, brought by a ship from Argier; and it is also carried to Hambrough. The Duke says the King purposes to forbid any of their ships coming into the river.' By 31 October: 'The plague is much in Amsterdam, and we in fears of it here, which God defend.'

By 26 November, quarantine regulations had been imposed on shipping coming from Amsterdam and Hamburg, 'for thirty days, as Sir Rd. Browne expressed it in the order of the Council, contrary to the import of the word . . .' adds Pepys, displaying his erudition. News from abroad continued to give warnings of plague during 1664, but the war with Holland occupies most of the chroniclers' space (except, of course, Pepys, who was more concerned with Mrs. Bagwell at the time). At the beginning of December 1664 two people, said to be Frenchmen but probably just strangers to London, died in a house in Drury Lane, and the circumstances of the deaths prompted the authorities to send two physicians and a surgeon to investigate. They found the unmistakable tokens of plague.

By January 1664-5 the numbers of deaths in the poorer parishes was increasing with alarming rapidity, from the usual weekly average of about 240 to 394, 415, 474 . . . then there was a merciful slackening until June, when in St. Giles parish alone more than 100 people died of plague. Pepys had the unpleasant truth forced into his consciousness by this outbreak:

'This day (June 7th 1665), much against my will, I did in Drury Lane see two or three houses marked with a red cross upon the doors, and "Lord have mercy upon us" writ there; which was a sad sight to me, being the first of the kind that, to my remembrance, I ever saw. It put me into an ill conception of myself and my smell, so that I was forced to buy some roll-tobacco to smell to and chaw, which took away the apprehension.'

By July death was parading openly in the streets; Evelyn noted 1100 deaths in the week up to 16 July and 2000 in the following week, 4000 a week by 8 August and 5000 in the following week, and 10,000 weekly by 7 September.

'. . . however, I went all along the city and suburbs from Kent Street to St. James's, a dismal passage, and dangerous to see so many coffins exposed in the streets, now thin of people; the shops shut up, and all in mournful silence, not knowing whose turn it might be next . . .' And on 11 October, he added:

'To London, and went through the whole City, having occasion to alight out of the coach in several places about business of money, when I was environed with multitudes of poor pestiferous creatures begging alms: the shops universally shut up, a dreadful prospect!'

Business in the city had almost ceased: on 16 August Pepys recorded that two shops in three were shut up, and very few people remained. The universal fear of contamination pervaded everyone's behaviour—'Thence with a lanthorn, in great fear of meeting of dead corpses, carried to be buried; but, blessed be God, met none, but did see now and then a linke (which is the mark of them) at a distance.'

And Pepys again, on 22 August:

'. . . I went away and walked to Greenwich, in my way seeing a coffin with a dead body therein, dead of the plague, lying in an open close belonging to Coome farme, which was carried out last night and the parish have not appointed any body to bury it; but only set a watch there day and night, that nobody should go thither or come thence, which is a most cruel thing: this disease making us more cruel to one another than if we are doggs . . .'

All the notes on the time emphasize the melancholy system of shutting up houses. Once plague had been detected in a house, the premises were shut and guarded to prevent anyone coming in or going out: usually this meant that the sound perished with sick. The orders for this incarceration were published at the end of June 1665, to take effect from 1 July. After clauses concerning the appointment of examiners of bodies, watchmen, women searchers, and chirurgeons, these include the following regulations:

Orders Concerning Infected Houses and Persons Sick of the Plague

Notice to be given of the Sickness
The master of every house, as soon as any one in his house complaineth, either of blotch or purple, or swelling in any part of his body, or falleth otherwise dangerously sick, without apparent cause of some other disease, shall give knowledge thereof to the examiner of health within two hours after the said sign shall appear.

Sequestration of the Sick
As soon as any man shall be found by this examiner, chirurgeon, or searcher to be sick of the plague, he shall the same night be sequestered in the same house; and in case he be so sequestered, then, though he afterwards die not, the house wherein he sickened shall be shut up for a month, after the use of the due preservatives taken by the rest. . . .

Shutting up of the House
If any person shall have visited any man known to be infected of the plague, or entered willingly into any known infected house, being not allowed, the house wherein he inhabiteth shall be shut up for certain days by the examiner's direction. . . .

Every visited House to be marked
That every house visited be marked with a red cross of a foot long in the middle of the door, evident to be seen, and with these usual printed words, that is to say, 'Lord, have mercy upon us', to be set close over the same cross, there to continue until lawful opening of the same house.

One good enactment, had it only been carried out, was the resolve of the city authorities to keep the streets cleaner:

ORDERS FOR CLEANSING AND KEEPING OF THE STREETS SWEET

The Streets to be kept Clean
First, it is thought necessary, and so ordered, that every householder do cause the street to be daily prepared before his door, and so to keep it clean swept all the week long.

That Rakers take it from out the Houses
That the sweeping and filth of houses be daily carried away by the rakers, and that the raker shall give notice of his coming by the blowing of a horn, as hitherto hath been done.

Laystalls to be made far off from the City
That the laystalls be removed as far as may be out of the city and common passages, and that no nightman or other be suffered to empty a vault into any garden near about the city.

Care to be had of unwholesome Fish or Flesh, and of musty Corn
That special care be taken that no stinking fish, or unwholesome flesh, or musty corn, or other corrupt fruits of what sort soever, be suffered to be sold about the city, or any part of the same.

That the brewers and tippling-houses be looked unto for musty and unwholesome casks.

That no hogs, dogs, or cats, or tame pigeons, or conies, be suffered to be kept within any part of the city, or any swine to be or stray in the streets or lanes, but that such swine be impounded by the beadle or any other officer, and the owner punished according to the Act of Common Council, and that the dogs be killed by the dog-killers appointed for that purpose.

The orders then go on to forbid begging, plays, bear-baiting, singing of ballads, buckler-play, public feasting, disorderly tippling, and frequenting coffee-houses after nine o'clock at night. It is a pity that the clerks who drew up these rules for Sir John Lawrence, Lord Mayor, and Sir George Waterman and Sir Charles Doe, Sheriffs, did not go further and specify the exact degree of disorderliness in the tippling that should merit punishment: in other parts of the document, one is struck with helpless wonder at the cold-blooded bureaucratic mind that could specify the size of the red cross, and the wording of the notice, that spelled a dreadful death for whole households.

'The shutting up of houses was at first counted a very cruel and un-Christian method, and the poor people so confined made bitter lamentations. Complaints of the severity of it were also daily brought to my Lord Mayor, of houses causelessly (and some maliciously) shut up.'*

The same severe policies were adopted all over the country, and anyone unfortunate enough to fall ill, from whatever cause and with any symptoms even slightly resembling plague, kept the matter quiet for as long as possible. Otherwise, at the earnest request of his neighbours, he might find his house shut up and his household imprisoned. Sir Richard Fanshawe, travelling in Ireland, must have had an unpleasant shock one morning on awaking:

'. . . as soon as my husband had put on his gown and began to put on his stockings, he called me saying "my heart, what great spots are these on my legs? Sure, it is the plague. But I am very well, and feel nothing." At which I ran out of the bed to him, and saw my own legs in the same condition; and upon examining the cause we found that the sheets being short and the blankets full of fleas, we had those spots made by them.'†

Conditions in houses of the time did nothing to discourage rats and their attendant fleas, so that plague spread despite all the regulations. Sanitation was as bad as ever, or even deteriorating in the towns, as the population and the degree of overcrowding increased, and the perennial problem of waste disposal received its perennial answer:

'October 20th 1660. This morning one came to advise with me where to make me a window into my cellar in lieu of one which Sir W. Batten had stopped up, and going down into my cellar to look I stepped into a great heap of ——, by which I found that Mr. Turner's house of office is full and comes into my cellar, which do trouble me, but I shall have it helped. . . .'‡

* Defoe.
† *Memoirs of Ann, Lady Fanshawe*, 1600–72.
‡ Pepys.

Samuel was rather fastidious for his day: less fond of dogs than his king (Charles II was tolerant of dogs, and the court habitually stank of them), he threatened to throw his wife's dog 'which her brother gave her' out of the window if it made any more messes in the house. On another occasion he confined it to the cellar for the same reason—presumably the dog could make little difference to the inroads already made by Mr. Turner's privies.

On the other hand, in case of necessity, Pepys's notions of etiquette were different from those of Emily Post:

'September 28th 1665 . . . and so I to bed, and in the night was mightily troubled with a looseness (I suppose from some fresh damp linen that I put on this night), and feeling for a chamber-pott, there was none, I having called the mayde up out of her bed, she had forgot I suppose to put one there; so I was forced in this strange house to rise and shit in the chimney twice; and so to bed and was very well again . . .'

The absence of privies was a constant worry: on one occasion Samuel records having to pretend an appointment at the Harp and Ball in order to ease himself on the way home, and Elizabeth, his wife, was unlucky enough to have a colic when they visited the Duke of York's playhouse—'so I was forced to go out of the house with her to Lincoln's Inn walks, and there in a corner she did her business, and was by and by well, and so into the house again . . .' For the less squeamish there was the open street:

'One day goeing on foote to Guild-hall with his Clarke behind him, he was surprised in Cheapside with a sudden and violent Loosenesse, neer the Standard. He turned up his breech against the Standard and bade his man hide his face; For they shall never see my Arse again, sayd he.'*

It is a wonder that Pepys was not more troubled by this sort of accident, for he is constantly complaining of colic, which he tended to blame on such foolish practices as washing his feet. Elizabeth Pepys rarely took such risks:

'February 21st, 1664–5 . . . my wife being busy in going with her woman to a hot-house to bathe herself, after her long being within doors in the dirt, so that she now pretends a resolution of being hereafter very clean. How long it will hold I can guess . . .'

* Aubrey, *Brief Lives*, Sir William Fleetwood.

This was unfair. Elizabeth had washed herself thoroughly on 21 November 1660, before being presented to the Queen: so thoroughly, in fact, that Sam retired to bed before she had finished the process. And in any case, washing must have been a thankless task for poor Elizabeth. The house was continually in a state of disorder from the streams of carpenters and painters called in by Samuel to alter a door here, stairs there, as his income and perquisites as Secretary to the Navy increased, and his ideas on suitable home comforts grew more expansive. Even Samuel noticed the dirt caused by these upheavals, and he has set in his diary many contributions to the literature on the faults of the British Workman, but Elizabeth and her succession of maids had to clean up the dirt and rubbish. The constant coming and going of friends and business clients must also have added to the dirt, especially on the floors. Pepys and his friends were not yet of the class who habitually used carriages, although they might for a special occasion. Most of the time they walked, and as the London streets were foul for most of the year, with beaten mud, rubbish, offal, and contributions from Sir William Fleetwood and his like, this must have meant a constant battle against filth tracked into the house.

If possible, hygiene seems to have been worse among the very rich than among the middle classes. Anthony à Wood, describing the removal of Charles II and some of his court to Oxford to avoid the plague, was forced to admit that, noble or not, they were 'nasty and beastly' in their personal habits. They left 'excrements in every corner, in chimneys, studies, cole-houses, cellars'. No doubt Charles's dogs contributed their share. There are again traces of that curious attitude that a 'manly' man did not concern himself about hygiene, leaving such matters to women and fops. In Etherege's *The Man of Mode*, the comic character is Sir John Fopling Flutter, who washes and uses perfume. The manly character is Dorimant, who, when offered essence of orange-flower water, says indignantly, 'I will smell as I do today, no offence to the ladies' noses.' This attitude is surprisingly prevalent even today—asked his opinion of an after-shave lotion, one latter-day Dorimant commented sourly, 'A *man* should only smell of three things—sweat, tobacco, and alcohol.' The Restoration man had an even wider spectrum of odours.

As bodily functions were a good deal more public than they are now, it is not surprising that they figured more openly in public humour.

'1659–60 February 7th ... Mr Moore told me of a picture hung up at the Exchange of a great pair of buttocks shooting of a turd into Lawson's mouth, and over it was wrote "The thanks of the house". Boys do now cry "Kiss my Parliament", instead of "Kiss my rump", so great and general a contempt is the Rump come to among all the good and bad.'*

Such functions could even figure in civic ceremony. Marmeduke Rawdon, who died in February 1688–9, left an unusual contribution to the York civic plate: £60 for a gold chain for the 'Lady Maioresse' and £10 to provide a silver chamber-pot for the Lord Mayor, inscribed 'The Gift of Marmeduke Rawdon Merchant of London, Sonne of Laurence Rawdon late Alderman of this City. anno 1672'. An ungrateful city keeps this elegant piece of work separate from the rest of the civic plate, and there does not appear to be any appropriate ceremony for occasions when new Lord Mayors take it into their charge. It should at least serve as a reminder that, among the many charms of Jacobean York, there is a background of 'nasty and beastly' sanitation.

One far-sighted man saw the connection between plague and the filth of the cities. Richard Mead, M.D., Physician to St. Thomas's Hospital, was born too late to see the Great Plague, but he observed it as it continued in Europe, and he saw the ravages of other epidemics, like the return of sweating sickness in the guise of 'Dunkirk fever'. He wrote a treatise on the treatment of epidemics, *A Short Discourse concerning Pestilential Contagion and the Methods to be used to Prevent it*, which was published in 1720, but which deals largely with the great epidemics of the century before. Mead was all for cleaning up the cities:

'It has besides been remarked in all Times, that the Stinks of *stagnating Waters* in Hot Weather, *putrid Exhalations* from the Earth; and above all, the Corruption of dead *Carcasses* lying unburied, have occasioned *infectious Diseases*.'

He disapproved of the custom of shutting up plague-infected houses, believing rightly that this merely incubated the disease in more people:

* Pepys.

(Overseers of the Poor) 'should visit the Dwellings of all the meaner sort of the Inhabitants, and where they find them *stifled up too close* and *nasty*, should lessen their number by sending some into better Lodgings, and should take Care, by all manner of Provision and Encouragement, to make them more *cleanly* and *sweet* . . . It is of more Consequence to be observed, that as *Nastiness* is a great source of *Infection*, so *Cleanliness* is the greatest Preservative: Which is the true Reason, why the Poor are most obnoxious to Disasters of this Kind.'

Mead suggested lazarettos at ports capable of keeping sailors for a full forty-day quarantine, clothes of infected people to be burned, and the clothes of people exposed to the disease to be aired in the sun (a very early example of ultra-violet ray sterilization). With considerable foresight of modern views on psychosomatic effects, he pointed out that despair and loss of morale made people more susceptible to disease, and recommended that every step should be taken by the authorities to avoid 'dejection of Spirits' among the citizens. Small wonder that his views, and his book, seemed to have sunk into obscurity without even a ripple on the surface of civic complacency. The streets remained dirty, carcasses remained unburied, waters stagnated, and the houses of the poor remained stifled up too close and nasty. When a cure came for London's plague-sores, it was far more drastic and savage—a cautery.

'1666 September 2nd (Lord's day). Some of our mayds sitting up late last night to get things ready against our feast today, Jane called us up about three in the morning, to tell us of a great fire they saw in the City. So I rose and slipped on my night-gowne, and went to her window, and thought it to be on the back-side of Marke-Lane at the farthest; but being unused to such fires as followed, I thought it far enough off; and so went to bed again and to sleep . . .'

Pepys went in the morning to see the fire, and was amazed by its extent. With the eye of a reporter of genius, he noted down the odd details of the holocaust:

'. . . Everybody endeavouring to remove their goods, and flinging into the river or bringing them into lighters that lay off; poor people staying in their houses as long as till the very fire touched them, and then running into boats, or clambering from one pair of stairs by the waterside to another. And among other things, the poor pigeons, I perceive, were loth to leave their houses, but hovered about the windows and balconys till they were, some of them burned, their wings, and fell down . . .'

The fire burned until 6 September.

'They came to nothing near this, which in three days and three nights, of about 460 acres of ground upon which the City of London stood, hath swept away about 350, which is at the rate of four parts in five; having destroyed about 12,000 houses, eighty-seven parochial churches,' said *Rege Sincera*, the pseudonymous author of *Observations, both Historical and Moral, upon the Burning of London 1666*, adding a list of the causes of the fire:

'. . . as in this sad and lamentable Fire, we see the carelessness of a baker, the solitariness and darkness of the night, the disposition of old and ruinous buildings, the narrowness of the streets, the abundance of combustible and bituminous matter, the foregoing summer extraordinarily hot and dry, a violent easterly wind, and the want of engines and water, concur as it were unanimously to the production of this wonderful conflagration and to do in four days what four armies of enemies (not opposed) could scarce have done in eight. . .'

The fire caused a great solemnity among Londoners and others. More dramatic than the plague, and, for the devout, a dreadful premonstration of the wrath to come, it called forth sermons and commentaries in language worthy of King James's Bible.

'The glory of God is now fled away like a bird, the trade of London is shattered and broken into pieces; her delights also are vanished, and pleasant things laid waste. Now no chanting to the sound of the viol, and dancing to the sweet music of other instruments. And the habitations of many who fear God have not escaped; and in the places where God hath been served, and his servants have lived, now nettles are growing, owls are screeching, and cut-throats are lurking,' said the Rev. Thomas Vincent. John Evelyn, more concerned with laying the blame than regretting the facts, noted on 10 October:

'This day was ordered a general fast through the nation, to humble us on the late dreadful conflagration, added to the plague and war, the most dismal judgements that could be inflicted; but which indeed we highly deserved for our prodigious ingratitude, burning lusts, dissolute court, profane and abominable lives, under such dispensations of God's continued favour in restoring Church, Prince, and People from our late intestine calamities, of which we were altogether unmindful, even to astonishment. This made me resolve to go to our parish assembly . . .'

Evelyn must have written this salutary diatribe while in the course of his great plan for rebuilding the city. He had been appointed to make a survey of the ruins, and pointed out the folly of continuing to build in wood, in a crowded city. This recommendation, with such an object lesson so recently taught, bore fruit:

'The woeful experience in this late heavy visitation hath sufficiently convinced all men of the pernicious consequences which have attended the building with timber, and even with stone itself, and the notable benefit of brick, which in so many places hath resisted and even extinguished the Fire: and we do hereby declare our express will and pleasure, that no man whatsoever shall presume to erect any house or building, great or small, but of brick or stone; and if any man shall do the contrary, the next magistrate shall forthwith cause it to be pulled down, and such farther course shall be taken for his punishment as he deserves.'*

Not every house was rebuilt with brick or stone, of course, but sufficient of the new buildings were made of masonry for the 'notable benefit of brick' to be felt, not only in the greater fire-resistance foreseen by Evelyn and Wren, but in other ways which they could not have recognized. Removal of the timber-framed houses made life far more difficult for the rats in the city. Where before they had had easy access to houses and food stores, simply by gnawing the wood away, they now found uneatable barriers. At the same time, the native black rat (*Mus rattus*) was already engaged in fierce competition with the larger and more combative brown rat (*Mus norvegicus*) for the available feeding places, and the rebuilding hastened the process by which the brown rats, introduced from ships, drove out their smaller and blacker cousins. All rats carry fleas, but the black rat is happier in houses where there are human beings, and therefore tends to be a more dangerous plague-carrier. The brown rat does not like the disturbance caused by human

* Royal Proclamation, Sept., 1666.

94

inhabitants, and prefers to live in buildings that are not inhabited, such as warehouses and stores. London reaped the benefit of this ecological change, and the plague was virtually eliminated from the city.

The outbreak of 1665–6 was in fact the last *epidemic* of plague in Britain. The 'cure' in London had been savage and costly, but why plague should have died out in other places is obscure. York, Bristol, Norwich, and the other large towns had fires regularly, but nothing to match the London holocaust, and Bristol in particular was still a filthy city, and remained so for a century afterwards. However, we must remember that even in 1666 London and its immediate suburbs contained almost one-fifth of the total population, and most of the epidemic diseases tended to start from the 'Great Wen'. In Bristol, a busy seaport, brown rats had already dominated the black variety, and this may also have helped to eliminate the plague. Whatever the exact reasons, one chapter in the history of dirt and disease in England was over.

9. *The Yahoos*

Like house-agents' prospectuses and architects' 'impressions', city plans tend to dwell on the broad architectural features, almost the ideals, of their subject, and to ignore the unpleasant little realities that human beings introduce. The aftermath of the Great Fire produced a great flock of city planners and map-makers: in London they could display each new triumph of the rebuilding, and in other cities they could record the anxiety of the provincial gentry to keep pace with their London counter-parts.

True, London was not the cosmopolis planned by Christopher Wren or John Evelyn in their optimistic drawings. No mere architects or surveyors, however respected, could cut through the gold tape of property ownership. Wren and Evelyn might have the ear of Charles II, but Charles was too wise to antagon-ize the landowners and the City merchants just for the sake of a little town planning. Nevertheless, throughout the city, among the untidy litter of crowded houses, the beginning of the eighteenth century saw beautiful individual buildings—St. Bride's in Fleet Street, St. Mary-le-Bow, the new Westminster Palace—and on Ludgate Hill the workmen were just starting work on the great dome of the new St. Paul's, the masterpiece of the Surveyor of the Royal Works, to make a timeless monu-ment to elegance and reason.

The panoramas of the city published by S. and N. Buck in 1749 show the extent of the transformation. The spires created by Wren and Hawksmoor blossom above the roofs of new houses; solid masonry has replaced the timber and plaster of the last two centuries. Even in areas which escaped the fire, it became the mark of a successful man to pull down the old half-timbered house and put up one in the new style. The streets are even (a very little) wider, and the overhanging upper storeys are disappearing fast as houses are rebuilt or refaced. Metro-politan pleasures—the club, the coffee-house, the theatre—are extending all over the town. It was a great city, with nearly 700,000 inhabitants in 1700. These are not shown on the city plans, but they left their traces.

The Bucks' panoramas are drawn from a viewpoint on the riverside, and the houses of watermen, chandlers, dealers, and all the other trades who live on, or by, the river are crowded down to the water's edge. At intervals in the engravings there appear large misshapen lumps, about as big as a fair-sized house, and hatched over by the engraver as if they were meant to depict thatched dwellings, or some other structure dressed with straw. One of these is prominent just east of Brown's Wharf, near the site of the present Southwark Bridge, another is at Whitefriar's Wharf, just west of Blackfriar's Bridge, and a third huge structure stands just next to Puddle Dock, by the site of the existing Mermaid Theatre. The name of the last area helps to identify these mysterious features of the city: it is called Dung Wharf, and the huge amorphous mounds, set snugly among the houses by the river, are laystalls, areas for piling the dung and other sweepings from the streets, and the cartloads of muck taken out of privies. Laystalls proliferated on the outskirts of every town and city, piling up until someone decided that it would be profitable to cart the dung out into the country and sell it to farmers. The riverside heaps in London were usually cleared into barges, like that met by Ben Jonson's travellers, and taken up the river to the market gardens of Pimlico and Victoria, thus helping to provide the fresh vegetables for the citizens of London and Westminster. From the ecologist's point of view, the constant circulation of nitrogen which this system represented was admirable, but the process must have seemed less pleasant to the inhabitants of the streets leading to the laystalls and the houses which stood on every side of them. Fortunately the feelings of such people did not matter very much: Strype dismisses the subject in his 1755 survey of London by saying that only 'the most ordinary people' lived in the streets around the dungheaps.

Waste disposal for the more distant parts of the city was more difficult. Dung collection was a commercial enterprise, and carriage by barge was cheap, so the streets near the Thames were cleansed fairly often; however, it was hardly worth the effort to cart dung all the way from Holborn, for example, to the river, and the Fleet River was becoming more and more difficult to navigate. Fortunately there were some collectors who established a trade with the farmers and market gardeners to the north of London, and the rest of the rubbish tended to find its way, very slowly, to the great heaps that stood around the edges of the city.

> 'You recollect the cinder heap,
> Vot stood in Gray's Inn Lane, sirs?'

asks 'Adam Bell, the Literary Dustman' nostalgically in a late Georgian ballad. In fact, the heap was not only of cinders, but ashes, rubble, crumbling plaster and rotting wood, exhausted tan bark and other trade waste, offal, vegetable scraps, and the emptying of tens of thousands of chamber-pots. An affluent society had not yet produced the wide variety of rubbish that we can boast today, but the eighteenth-century citizens contributed what they could. The pile started as a convenient dump for the rubble when the debris of the Great Fire was being cleared away, but it continued to grow, and by about 1780 it had spread to cover $8\frac{1}{2}$ acres, the whole of the area now bounded by Grays Inn Road, Euston Road, and Argyle Street. It was finally cleared away because the rubbish acquired an unexpected commercial value: the owner of the land sold the heap to Russia as material for the rebuilding of Moscow after the destruction of 1812. The heap is still commemorated, however, in Laystall Street, which runs into the Clerkenwell Road.

If the householder were lucky, there might be either the Thames or one of London's other innumerable waterways to help with his sewage disposal problems. The Fleet Ditch had been widened after the Great Fire, cleared of some of the accumulated filth that had impeded the movement of the water, and given a new and impressive outlet to the Thames. The new portion was entitled the Fleet Canal, but the name did not stick, nor was the canal a commercial success. Habit dies hard, and when the choice lies between throwing your rubbish into the street or throwing it into the canal, most householders chose the canal, with the heartfelt support of all the pedestrians. The same disposal system applied to any other embarrassing material:

> . . . the Fleet Ditch with disembogueing streams
> Rolls the large tribute of dead dogs to Thames . . .

comments Pope in the *Dunciad*, and there seem to have been enough dead dogs to encourage a grisly trade.

'On Tuesday the body of a young fellow was left by the tide in the Fleet Ditch. As he was in his waistcoat and without shoes, it was generally believed that he was robbed and murdered. But, since, it appears that he was one who used to traverse the common sewer in search of dead dogs for the benefit of their skins.'*

Apparently the young man had been pursuing his trade in the closed-over part of the Ditch, and was caught by the tide coming up the Canal. The Canal portion was finally filled in and became New Bridge Street. One side of the impressive entry is now occupied by Unilever House.

Despite the filth of the water, young men still occasionally bathed in the Fleet Ditch, incredible though it may seem. Pope, in a characteristic image, points out how useful this training in literal muckraking will be if they intend to embark on a study of the newspapers of the day:

> Here strip my children! Here at once leap in!
> Here prove who best can dash thro' thick and thin,
> And who the most in love of dirt excel,
> Or dark dexterity of groping well.
> Who flings most filth, and wide pollutes around
> The stream, be his the Weekly Journals, bound.†

And if you did not live by a convenient river? Well, as always, there was the street. If you were out of doors, any corner or doorway could be used in emergency. The eighteenth-century

---

* *London Penny Post*, 22 December, 1749.
† *Dunciad*, II, 263–8.

citizen could not afford to be embarrassed by such an event, any more than his counterpart of the previous century, and many citizens followed the example of Sir William Fleetwood or Mrs. Pepys. For those who were more refined or modest, or who could not find a convenient corner in Lincoln's Inn Walks, there were even street traders—in Edinburgh, for example, one such benefactor to distressed humanity would allow you the use of his bucket and a cloak to put round you for a small fee: his cry was 'Wha wants me for a bawbee?' In the house, there were pots, but the problem of emptying them had not been solved.

'Do not carry down the necessary Vessels for the Fellows to see, but empty them out of the Window, for your Lady's Credit. It is highly improper for Men Servants to know that fine Ladies have occasion for such Utensils; and do not scour the Chamberpot, because the smell is wholesome . . .' advised Swift, in his *Directions to Servants*, which seems to have been written with a pen dipped in something worse than vitriol.

Not only chamber-pots were emptied into the streets, although there were enough of these. Offal from butchers' slaughter-houses, waste from tanneries, trimmings from vegetables and meat, fish heads, eel skins, and any food which had decayed too far even for those robust stomachs, all was shot into the kennel, the gutter that ran down the middle of each street. Unless a scavenger found some part of the rubbish useful, it might lie there for days, rotting, until rain came to carry it away, or at least transfer it from one street to another. This made walking in towns after rain as hazardous as walking at night:

> Now from all parts the swelling kennels flow,
> And bear their trophies with them as they go:
> Filth of all hues and odours seem to tell
> What street they sailed from, by their sight and smell . . .
> Sweepings from butchers' stalls, dung, guts, and blood,
> Drown'd puppies, shaking sprats, all drenched in mud,
> Dead cats, and turnip-tops, come tumbling down the flood.*

When necessity drove 'the better sort of folk' to walk the streets, they used pattens, a kind of wooden galosh designed to keep the feet two or three inches off the ground: even this was

* *Tatler*, 17 October, 1710.

not always high enough, as many of the streets were four or five inches deep in wet, slimy mud after rain.

The growth of population, especially in London (nearly 700,000 in 1700 to 900,000 in 1800), meant that the old methods of rubbish disposal could not cope with the increasing load of sewage, food waste, and household and trade rubbish. London was bad, but some of the other large cities were worse. Bristol, despite the advantages of a sea channel for disposal, had streets even fouler than the worst London alleys, mainly because they were so narrow. In most Bristol streets it was impossible to take a cart through, and sledges were used to carry goods about the town. Even at the beginning of the century, the great majority of town houses were overcrowded: ten to a room was common in Manchester.

In Edinburgh, as G. M. Trevelyan writes, in his *English Social History*, the early morning was a particularly hazardous time:

'Far overhead the windows opened, five, six, or ten storeys in the air, and the close stools of Edinburgh discharged the collected filth of the last twenty-four hours into the street. It was good manners for those above to cry "Gardy-loo!" (*Gardez l'eau*) before throwing. The returning roysterer cried back "Haud yer han", and ran with humped shoulders, lucky if his vast and expensive full-bottomed wig was not put out of action by a cataract of filth . . .'

The City Guard were supposed to clear the muck away, but rarely did so: characteristically in Presbyterian Scotland it was expressly forbidden to clear the streets on a Sunday, so that Edinburgh, like the early Church, had a deep knowledge of the odour of sanctity.

Some unpopular people, of course, might shout 'Haud yer han'' or its equivalent as much as they pleased, but they would still remain a legitimate target. The returning drunk in Hogarth's 'Night', for example, is Sir Thomas de Veil, a notoriously severe magistrate, going to his home in Leicester Square, so it is probable that the timing of the chamber-pot is a deliberate revenge by some aggrieved fellow-townsman.

Even in the country, where the open spaces and fresh air might have offered opportunities for a cleaner style of living, or at least decent disposal of sewage and rubbish, conditions among the poor were as bad as in the towns. There was the same

crowding, the same miserable conditions, and the same indifference to filth. In most country cottages the living accommodation was still shared with animals—chickens, pigs, even a
cow—while among the very poor the cost of shelter forced the
crowding of nine or ten people into each tiny cottage. In *The
Parish Register* Crabbe shows the true face of the pastoral idyll so
fashionable among his urban contemporaries:

> Between the road-way and the walls, offence
> Invades all eyes, and strikes on every sense;
> There lie, obscene, at every open door,
> Heaps from the hearth and sweepings from the floor,
> And day by day the mingled masses grow,
> As sinks are disembogued, and kennels flow.

A Gulliver visiting Britain in the early eighteenth century
might have regarded it as a nation, like the unfortunate
Richard the Raker, drowning in its own excrement.

Apart from the all-too-human filth, the cities were smoke-
blackened, and even the fine new buildings did not remain clean
for very long. Chimneys were still inefficient in the best houses,
and non-existent in the poorer ones. Lighting came from
candles made commercially from inedible tallow (which at this
period must have meant fat that was so rancid that its smell was
detectable even over the general background reek of the towns)
or were made at home from 'kitchen-stuff', basically rancid
dripping. As plaited wicks had not been invented, such candles
smoked abominably. Wax candles were used by the rich on
special occasions, but were too expensive for general or frequent
use. A few streets in London were lighted at night, but most of
the lamps consisted of pieces of rag soaked in fat rendered down
from offal, so the smoke and smell must have far exceeded the
light. Everything was grimed with soot: '. . . the Chimney-
Sweeper's cry Every blackening church appals' said Blake in
Songs of Experience, thus coupling the two main results of the
wasteful use of coal. Sir Christopher Wren, in equally pessi-
mistic terms, reported that even before St. Paul's was finished,
it was 'already so black with coal smoke that it has lost half its
elegance'. The first stone was laid in 1675, and by 1702 Wren
had to arrange for a 'special engine' to spray water over the
stonework in an attempt to clean it before a special Thanks-

giving service in the presence of Queen Anne. St. Paul's had to wait until 1968 for its elegance to be restored, with the help of the more efficient special engines of Messrs. Szerelmey Ltd., and a large public fund.

Not all the smoke was outside the buildings. John Evelyn, in his comments on town planning, had already in Charles II's time drawn attention to the pernicious effects of coal fires:

> One day, as I was walking in your Majesty's palace at Whitehall (where I have sometimes the honour to refresh myself with the sight of your illustrious presence, which is the joy of your people's hearts) that a presumptuous smoke, issuing from one or two tunnels (*chimneys*) near Northumberland House, and not far from Scotland Yard, did so invade the Court; that all the rooms, galleries, and places about it were filled and infested with it; and that to such a degree, as men could hardly discern one another for the cloud, and none could support, without manifest inconveniency. . . . This glorious and ancient City, which from wood might be rendered brick, and (like another Rome) from brick made stone and marble; which commands the proud ocean to the Indies, and reaches the farthest Antipodes, should wrap her stately head in the clouds of smoke and sulphur, so full of stink and darkness, I deplore with just indignation . . .*

In this smoky, stinking, cluttered environment only the eccentrics fought to keep clean. For the rich it was difficult enough, for the poor impossible. Clothes were washed rarely, and removed as little as possible, for fear of taking cold. Francis Place, early in the nineteenth century, set down memories of his youth with little relish:

'. . . the wives of journeymen, tradesmen and shopkeepers either wore leather stays or what were called full-boned stays . . . These were never washed although worn day by day for years. The wives and grown daughters of tradesmen, and gentlemen even, wore petticoats of camblet, lined with dyed linen, stuffed with wool and horsehair and quilted; these were also worn day by day till they were rotten.'

Part of the trouble was the cold. The English climate is not

* *Fumifugium, or the Inconvenience of the Aer and Smoak of London Dissipated,* 1661.

encouraging for the fresh-air life, but all the houses, except the very finest, were very draughty. Door and window frames, hand-cut, tended to gape and warp, and floorboards were rarely covered properly, so that draughts came up between the boards. Glass was fairly common in the better-class houses by 1700, but it was still expensive to replace if broken, and the poor usually blocked up their windows with paper or rags, preferring warmth to light. Under these conditions, it would have taken an uncommon degree of hardihood to remove a comfortable, if smelly, petticoat stuffed with wool. Most people, in winter at least, slept in some or all of their day clothes. Laurence Sterne, in *A Sentimental Journey*, writes of sharing his inn bedroom with a lady, and remarks on the 'window which had neither glass nor oil-paper in it to keep out the tempest of the night', and he must have been quite glad to accede to the lady's request (for her moral safety) that he 'Should lie in his black silk breeches all night'. Clothes were not expected to possess the sort of elegance that comes from cleaning and pressing, so the fact that the black silk breeches were Sterne's 'best' was of no account. It is hard to imagine a modern novel in which the hero would put on his best suit to go to bed, even to oblige the most charming lady.

The poor, of course, were too busy to bother about cleanliness. Finding food and shelter was a full-time occupation, and in any case, if you have only the clothes you stand up in, you do not lightly embark on the business of washing them, especially in cold water and with no fire to dry them. 'Taking cold' usually meant death: in an environment where smallpox, typhus, typhoid, cholera, and 'London ague' (a kind of malaria that affected, among others, Oliver Cromwell and Charles II) made sure that only one child in four or five survived, a feverish cold could be the first sign of any one of several revolting deaths. Chills were avoided like the plague that was still a vivid and terrible memory.

Some enthusiasts washed their hands and faces, although even this presented difficulties. Alderman Boydell, a respected and wealthy publisher who became Lord Mayor of London, had no water piped to his house, but used to walk every morning to the public pump in Ironmonger Lane, solemnly place his huge wig on top of it, and then douse his head under the spout.

The water supply, where it existed, was intermittent. In

London, and other large cities, houses that were up-to-date enough to have water pipes were allowed a supply of water for two or three hours on about three days a week, so that they could fill their wooden storage tanks. Ball-valves were introduced about 1748, and saved the householder from missing his supply if he forgot to turn on the tap, and also the more serious consequences if he forgot to turn it off again when the tank was full. With such a limited supply of water, waste was taken very seriously. The mains through which water was supplied were tree-trunks bored down the centre and fastened together with iron hoops: they usually fitted so badly that about a quarter of the water was lost on the way through leakage. Another source of loss was the depredations of piratical citizens who secretly bored holes in the mains and inserted their own pipes, or 'quills', to get a supply of water without paying for it. The use of more than one's share was frowned upon even for subscribers. A Mr. Melmoth of Bath, who was enterprising enough to fit a water-closet in his house in 1770, had his water supply cut off until he removed the wasteful device.

The water itself was of doubtful quality. Strype, in his modernized version of Stow's *Survey of London* published in 1720 and 1755, remarks ominously that Thames water is superior to New River water because the sediment settles more rapidly. In York the water was so cloudy that householders who could manage to do so kept it for several days in large pots or tanks, to allow the mud to settle. Brewers seemed more critical of their water supply than most other users, and several London brewers joined together to invest in a long pipe going right out into the middle of the Thames to collect their water. This was obviously a good move when so many people drank small beer in preference to the doubtful water supply.

Some users relied on the private water works. These depended on pumps to raise the water from the rivers, and the pumps, until the advent of steam power, were driven by waterwheels powered from the river flow. The London Bridge Waterworks was one of the mechanical wonders of the age, with 20-ft-diameter wheels that could be raised or lowered to suit the state of the tide, and which rotated six times per minute at full tide, working a series of pumps that could raise 123,120 gallons of water to a height of 120 feet in one hour. Less wonderful, but perhaps more remarkable, were Marchant's Waterworks in London, on the corner of St. Martin's Lane and Chandos Street (a site which is now occupied by the Coliseum Theatre). With more ingenuity than prudence, the pumps in this establishment, raising water from an inlet of the Thames, were powered by the nearest moving stream of liquid, which happened to be the flow from the main sewer. From contemporary descriptions it seems fairly certain that the outgoing sewage was discharged from the waterwheels into the same channel as the incoming water supply, making the whole process somewhat cyclic. Marchant's company must have been conscious that there was something a little objectionable about their process, because they embarked on the well-known commercial gambit, in such circumstances, of attacking *another* water-company for supplying contaminated water.

It is not entirely surprising that people used as little water as possible. M. de Saussure, a Swiss visitor to London in 1726, was astonished to see how little water was consumed for any purpose, and by the fact that the lower classes, even the paupers, never quenched their thirst with it. However, Dr. Lucas, in his *Essay on Waters* of 1756 comments that London is supplied with water 'in greater variety and abundance than any other city in Europe'. 'Abundance' sounds admirable, but 'variety', applied to water, is not so reassuring. He performed a simple analysis on the waters from the four main sources: the Thames (at the London Bridge Waterworks), the New River, Hampstead Ponds (from which water was piped to parts of north London) and a spring at the end of Rathbone Place. By boiling samples dry and weighing the solid residue he was able to find the amounts of dissolved material per gallon in each sample. From the Thames water he obtained $16\frac{1}{2}$ grains per gallon, from the New River $14\frac{1}{2}$ grains, from Hampstead Ponds 90 grains and from Rathbone Place 100 grains. The results for the Thames and the New River are reasonable, considering the natural hardness of London water, but one wonders exactly what was in the other two samples.

With such limited supplies of water, and the doubtful quality of much of the water that was available, bathing as a habit (or even as an event at all) had little chance of developing. Celia Fiennes noted with wonder that as early as 1700 Chatsworth had a 'batheing room' fitted with '2 locks to let in one hott, the other cold water to attemper it as persons please', but this must have been an extremely rare luxury. The only places where bathing was popular were the seaside resorts, at least after about 1730, and the spas.

Sea bathing at 'Brighthelmstone' is first recorded in 1736, but Dr. Russell, author of *A Dissertation Concerning the Use of Sea-Water in Diseases of the Glands*, popularized it after he settled in Brighton in 1754. It was a strictly medical practice, not intended to be indulged in for pleasure or even for cleanliness. Fanny Burney, Mrs. Thrale and the Misses Thrale bathed at Brighton before dawn in November, which does not suggest a very sybaritic occupation.

The spas were even more stringent in their methods, though to do them justice they were endeavouring to cure a very wide variety of ills. In *The Queen's Wells (That is, A Treatise on the Nature and Vertues of Tunbridge Water)*, Lodowick Rowzer, Doctor of Physick practising at Ashford, Kent, had already claimed that Tunbridge water was 'good for obstructions, agues, dropsy, black and yellow jaundice, schirrus binis or hard swelling of the spleen, scurvy, greensickness, whites in women, and defect and excess of their courses'. This was in 1670. By 1707, Dr. Joseph Browne had even more extravagant claims for bathing, and by far the most catchy title for his monograph: *An Account of the Wonderful Cures Performed by Cold Baths with Advice to the Water Drinkers at Tunbridge Wells, Hampstead, Astrope, Nasborough and all the Other Chalybeate Spaws Wherein the Usefulness of Cold Bathing is Further Recommended to Lovers of Coffee, Tea, Chocolate, Brandy etc.* Dr. Browne places more emphasis on 'cold' than 'bath'; for anyone with even the slightest genuine illness his methods must have represented kill or cure. On the other hand, many patients would have been glad to know that simple cold spring water could cure scrofula, rickets, mania, venereal diseases, and 'weakness of Erection, and a general disorder of the whole Codpiece Oeconomy'.

In the spas, and particularly at Bath, the main attraction was the social whirl, and as the town became more and more popular the results of overcrowding began to appear. Even in the previous century, Pepys had noted that in the Cross Bath:

'. . . though we designed to have done before company come,

much company come; very fine ladies; and the manner pretty enough, only methinks it cannot be clean to go so many bodies together in the same water . . .'

The doctors assured patients that the water could not transmit infection, and that the guides who led the bathers in and out of the water lived to a healthy old age. On the other hand, the satirist Ned Ward objected to the presence in the same bath of 'a buxom dame cleansing her *nunquam satis* from mercurial dregs and the remains of Roman vitriol' and another lady with 'more sores than Lazarus'. Fortunately the waters at Bath smell strongly of rotten eggs, so there was no question of annoyance from any other smell.

Drinking the water was a growing craze: some people drank several pints a day. Unfortunately, the Bath authorities did not see the necessity to keep a separate supply of water for this purpose. Christopher Anstey, in his *New Bath Guide* of 1766 describes the situation when the ladies of his Blunderhead family are 'taking the waters', while their maid Tabitha Runt is allowed as a special concession to enter the bath next door:

> You cannot conceive what a number of ladies
> Were washed in the water the same as our maid is . . .

which is perhaps only unseemly if you accept the conventions of the time that servants must be dirtier than gentlefolk, but later:

> So while little Tabby was washing her rump,
> The ladies kept drinking it out of the pump,

Which is a fairly delicate comment compared with Smollett's description of the pumped water in *Humphrey Clinker*:

'It is very far from being clear to me that the patients in the Pump Room don't swallow the scourgings of the bathers . . . in that case what a delicate beverage is every day quaffed by the drinkers; medicated with sweat and dirt and dandruff and the abominable discharges of various kinds, from twenty different diseased bodies, parboiling in the kettle below . . .'

Even in the spas there was economy in water, but had there been plenty it seems doubtful whether people elsewhere would have used it for bathing; the habit was too far removed from the notions of the time. To those few who had plenty of water, it was just a nuisance. A fascinating domestic crisis (or more a way of life) concerning water is revealed in a petition of 1750 directed to the aldermen of the City of London. A gentleman was appealing for the City to carry out their projected plans to bring proper drainage to the town: it emerged that the citizens of some areas were very much troubled by a number of small springs of water arising in the Norton Folgate district:

'Your petitioner well remembers every person in Spital Square in the Liberty of Norton Folgate greatly inconvenienced by the springs in the Liberty, insomuch that in his father's house there the water . . . used to be three or four feet deep in the cellars; and the servants used to punt themselves along in a washing tub from the cellar stairs to the beer-barrels to draw beer daily . . .'

These plans for proper drainage were a symptom of the urge for improvement that appeared towards the latter half of the century. Life had become so nauseous, especially in the towns, that even the strongly independent British realized that some collective action must be taken. Real efforts were made to enforce hitherto neglected regulations about street cleaning, to increase the supply of water and improve its quality, and to improve general sanitation. The water-closet, hitherto frowned upon as an expensive and wasteful luxury, began to appear more frequently in better-class homes.

John Aubrey had seen an early water-closet in 1678, at Sir Francis Carew's house in Beddington, Surrey, and describes it with a care that does him credit as a Fellow of the Royal Society, and also underlines the complete novelty of the idea:

'. . . a pretty machine to cleanse an House of Office, viz. by a small stream of water no bigger than one's finger, which ran into an engine made like a bit of a fire-shovel, which hung upon its centre of gravity, so that when it was full a considerable quantity of water fell down with some force.'

The was obviously self-operating, and not controlled by the user like Sir John Harington's 'Ajax': it would continue to flush automatically at intervals as long as the supply of water kept up. At Woburn, in 1748, the Duke of Bedford had four water-closets installed (though not, presumably, to attract visitors) of which, it was noted proudly, 'at least one is within the house'. The early models were followed by Banner's Patent Drain Trap, an ingenious device that had only one main fault—the patent trap tended to hinder the contents from going down the soil pipe when the closet was flushed, but presented no obstacle to foul air coming up the pipe all the rest of the time. However, it was no doubt more pleasant to use than an overflowing earth closet or a chamber-pot emptied out of the window into the street. In 1775 Alexander Cummings invented and patented a closet with an efficient trap to close the soil-pipe at all times except when the machine was actually flushing, and also introduced the U-trap. Joseph Bramah made some minor improvements to Cummings's design in 1778, and his model was so popular that his firm made 6,000 closets between 1778 and 1797.

Like all blessings, the water-closet had some unexpected disadvantages. As an advance in public hygiene, and as an improvement in the generally unpleasant standard of eighteenth-century life, its value was undeniable. But there was no concept of collective planning at the time (and if there had been, sectional interests would have stifled any effective action). Having designed a fairly reliable means for removing excrement from the houses of the well-to-do, the water-closet manufacturers did not see any responsibility to enquire where the sewage should go then. The closets mostly discharged into sewers or even open gutters running through the streets, and ultimately into the rivers. A large amount of sewage that had previously been confined to earth closets or carted away by nightmen for use on the land was now suddenly added to the already foul waterways. In London the Thames became so polluted, and the rise in demand for water-closets so great, that the end of the century saw an increase in the number of deaths from typhoid that paralleled the installation of the closets. In fact the death-rate, which had been falling with the advent of cleaner streets, more water, and the establishment of hospitals, rose again dramatically as the typhoid epidemic spread. They were not digging up Father's grave to build a sewer, but rather putting him in his grave before his time.

For the mass of the people, the eighteenth century closed little better than it had started. The efforts to improve conditions in the towns were largely offset by the explosive population growth. The total population of England and Wales increased from about 6½ million in 1750 to 9 million in 1800. With so many more people, the effects of overcrowding were intensified, the more abundant supplies of water had to go round further, and the pressure to dispose of rubbish wherever it could be shot meant that the streets were fouled as fast as they were cleansed. Many of the improvements of life did not reach the poor at all: the rich had the water-closets, the poor merely got more sewage in their drinking water. Life was short from the many endemic diseases, and it was also nasty and brutish to an extent that is difficult to imagine without nausea.

People found relief from their intolerable conditions in the most popular ways in any age—drinking, gambling, sex, and violence. Violence on the large scale was not common because of the rapid and savage means of repression, but on the small scale the streets of the towns, the highways, and the village greens were never free from violent crime: at night they were only frequented by drunks, fools, and those rich enough to pay their own bravos to protect them. Gambling was universal, but most flamboyant among the rich—Lord Chesterfield, that self-appointed model of the ideal man in an Age of Reason, almost left Bath, despite the fact that his 'cure' seemed to be working, because the stakes at the tables were too low to afford him any excitement.

Sex, in the promiscuous fashion of the day, led to its own hygiene problems. Boswell, among many others, found it better to wear his 'armour' when coupling with women in the Park, not for the purposes of contraception (which hardly entered the consciousness of a gentleman using a working-class woman) but to avoid venereal disease:

'At the bottom of the Haymarket I picked up a strong, jolly young damsel, and taking her under the arm I conducted her to Westminster Bridge, and then in armour complete did I engage her upon this noble edifice . . .* He was foolish enough to dispense with the armour when with his girl-friend Louisa, and as a consequence spent five miserable weeks confined to his rooms while being cured of gonorrhoea.

Drinking, however, was the universal panacea for the miseries of the day. Early in the century the art of distilling cheap gin had been made so simple and fool-proof that almost every

* Boswell, *London Journal*, 1762–3.

shopkeeper sold spirits; a loophole in the law made it possible for gin to be sold without a licence or any type of regulation, while beer was still only sold in licensed beershops, so the drinking of 'strong waters' became commoner than beer-drinking, and 'drunk for a penny, dead drunk for twopence' was almost literally true. Gin was the favoured spirit because it needed no maturing such as is given to brandy or whisky. Gin distilled today could be sold tomorrow, and even if it was a little raw, it was usually mixed with fruit cordials to make a palatable drink. At this period the consumption of cheap spirits in London, per head, was probably higher than at any time before or since.

Spirits make people indifferent or insensible to filth and wretchedness, but they also increase the filth and wretchedness. In an age when the sober man was forced by circumstances to have filthy habits, the drunk man became simply bestial. One dreadful story may serve as an example of the macabre effects which cheap gin could bring into the lives of the poor in the eighteenth century.

An Irishwoman, living in London, had a daughter who died of smallpox, a fairly common event at the time. The parish prepared with all speed to bury the girl in a pauper's grave, but the mother begged to be allowed to follow the traditional Irish custom of holding a wake and raising enough money from the mourners for a decent burial. She was allowed to keep the body at home. The wake was held, the mourners arrived, and the money was collected, but soon it began to slip away to provide more gin to keep the wake going, to stave off the awful morning-after. After a time they realized, blearily, that there was no money left for the funeral. So friends rallied round, and a second wake was held—with the same result.

Eventually the parish officers had to intervene to break up a scene that only Poe could have described adequately: a drunken orgy that had lasted for twelve days, a tiny filthy room packed with drunken, vomiting people—around a decomposing corpse, a fortnight dead. Smallpox was spreading from one mourner to another, and in the flicking light of the tallow dips it was impossible to tell whether the white-faced bodies lying on the floor were drunk, or diseased, or dead.

When we look at Georgian buildings, or read the Augustan couplets of Pope and Dryden, or see the costumes of the time, the eighteenth century seems a period of cool rationalism, detachment, dignity and proportion. If we then look deeper into the details of the lives of the mass of the people, the impression is more one of apes fighting and copulating on a dunghill. Even the costumes are a delusion: we see a lady's gown and wig, and think of the elegance of the ensemble, forgetting that the wig would be alive with vermin and the dress never washed. We see the amusing patches, and forget that they hid pimples, sores, and smallpox scars. We see one of the more exotic hair creations, such as those described by the noted hairdresser Mr. Gilchrist, the Vidal Sassoon of his day, and imagine that such confections are the froth on the surface of an inventive and enterprising age.

So they may be, but a writer in the *London Magazine* in 1768 took another view:

> . . . I allude to the present prodigious, unnatural, monstrous, and dirty mode of dressing the hair, which, adorned with many jewels, makes them at once to shine and stink upwards. Attracted by my eyes to approach as near as I could to these beautiful creatures, I have soon been repelled by my nose and been obliged to retire to a respectful distance. For (I will speak it out) I had the honour of smelling in the most unsavoury manner very many heads of the first rank and condition. . . .
>
> . . . I went the other morning to make a visit to an elderly aunt of mine, when I found her tendering her head to the ingenious Mr. Gilchrist, who has lately obliged the public with a most excellent essay upon hair. He asked her how long it was since her head had been opened or repaired. She answered, not above nine weeks. To which he replied, that was as long as a head could well go in the summer, and that therefore it was proper to deliver it now; for he confessed that it began to be a little *hazarde*.

(There follows a discussion on Mr. Gilchrist's names for the various styles in which the aunt may care to have her head of hair rebuilt.)

> When Mr. Gilchrist opened my aunt's head, as he called it, I must confess its effluvias affected my sense of smelling

disagreeably, which stench, however, did not surprize me
when I observed the great variety of materials employed in
raising the dirty fabrick. False locks to supply the great
deficiency of native hair, pomatum with profusion, greasy
wool to bolster up the adopted locks, and gray powder to
conceal at once age and dirt, and all these caulked together
by pins of an indecent length and corresponding colour.
When the comb was applied to the natural hair, I observed
swarms of animalculas running about in the utmost conster-
nation and in different directions, upon which I put my chair
a little further from the table and asked the operator whether
that numerous swarm did not from time to time send out
colonies to other parts of the body? He assured me that they
could not; for that the quantity of powder and pomatum
formed a glutinous matter, which like lime twigs to birds,
caught and clogged the little natives and prevented their
migration . . .

It was not only the fleas that wriggled. In the slums of St.
Giles, the inhabitants fought for space: 'Only at night can
their redundant numbers find room: for as long as they are
lively enough to turn and be aware of anything that presses
them, there is squeezing and jostling, and grumbling and
cursing.' The dense mass of houses, 'so olde they only seemen
not to falle' were in constant a turmoil, as sub-letting extended
down to rent for half a bed.

It was a time of cynicism and misanthropy, but most of the
misanthropes, like Chesterfield and Pope, turned their eyes
away from the filth around them, and only acknowledged its
existence with an occasional sneer or even an improving
anecdote—like Lord Chesterfield in 1747:

'I knew a gentleman who was so good a manager of his time,
that he would not even lose that small portion of it, which the
call of nature obliged him to pass in the necessary house; but
gradually went through all the Latin poets, in those moments.
He bought, for example, a common edition of Horace, of which
he tore off gradually a couple of pages, carried them with him
to that necessary place, read them first, and then sent them
down as a sacrifice to Cloacina.'

Others were practical and plain-spoken: it is pleasant to

find that John Wesley could ask without embarrassment, when planning a preaching tour in 1769; 'I particularly desire wherever you have preaching . . . that there may be a little-house.' Or perhaps he found that his preaching moved more than the spirit.

But there was one great misanthrope who could not forget the sad human condition. The human body and its functions fascinated and repelled Swift; he picks over the details of *The Lady's Dressing Room* like a surgeon faced with a particularly revolting deformity, appalled but professionally interested:

> But oh! it turn'd poor *Strephon's* Bowels,
> When he beheld and smelt the Towels,
> Begumm'd, bematter'd, and beslim'd
> With Dirt, and Sweat, and Ear-Wax grim'd.
> No Object *Strephon's* Eye escapes
> Here Petty coats in frowzy Heaps;
> Nor be the Handkerchiefs forgot
> All varnish'd o'er with Snuff and Snot . . .

and so on for 142 emetic lines.

In *Directions to Servants*, already mentioned, Swift sets down the dirtiest and most slatternly habits in the guise of advice to the household servants; to the butler, for instance:

'In bottling Wine, fill your Mouth full of Corks, together with a large plug of Tobacco, which will give to the wine the true Taste of the Weed, so delightful to all good Judges in drinking . . .'

(To the cook): 'You are to look upon your Kitchen as your Dressing Room; but, you are not to wash your Hands till you have gone to the Necessary-house, and spitted your Meat, trussed your Pullets, pickt your Sallad, nor indeed till after you have sent up the second Course; for your Hands will be ten times fouled with the many Things you are forced to handle; but when your Work is over, one Washing will serve for all . . .'

(To the footman): '. . . stick your Plate up to the Rim inclusive, in the left Side between your Waistcoat and your Shirt: this will keep it at least as warm as under your Armpit. . . . Never wear Socks when you wait at Meals, on the

Account of your own Health, as well as of them who sit at Table: because as most Ladies like the smell of young Men's Toes, so it is a sovereign Remedy against the Vapours.'

But this is mere playfulness compared with the view of humanity in the last part of *Gulliver's Travels*, 'A Voyage to the Country of the Houyhnhnms'. The Houyhnhnms, noble horses with every prudent virtue, are served by Yahoos, a dreadful caricature of human beings: filthy, stupid, violent and selfish. 'Upon the whole, I never beheld in all my travels so disagreeable an animal, nor one against which I naturally conceived so strong an antipathy.' The Yahoos, though they have dangerous teeth and nails, are too cowardly to use these against their masters or even Gulliver, and their main weapon is the hurling or dropping of their own excrement. When Gulliver first arrives on the island, they climb a tree and attack him in this way:

'. . . from whence they began to discharge their excrements on my head. However, I escaped pretty well by sticking close to the stem of the tree, but was almost stifled with the filth which fell about me on every side.'

When Gulliver catches a young Yahoo, his detestation becomes more acute:

'I observed the young animal's flesh to smell very rank, and the stink was somewhat between a weasel and a fox, but much more disagreeable. I forgot another circumstance (and perhaps I might have the reader's pardon, if it were wholly omitted), that while I held the odious vermin in my hands, it voided its filthy excrements of a yellow liquid substance, all over my clothes; but by good fortune there was a small brook hard by, where I washed myself as clean as I could, although I durst not come into my master's presence, until I were sufficiently aired.'

Gulliver's greatest shame arises when it is recognized by the Houyhnhnms that he is also a kind of Yahoo, similar in body and therefore presumed similar in degradation. In the end the Houyhnhnms tell him that he must leave their island because, despite his greater intelligence and attempts to improve his moral status, he is, after all, only a Yahoo—creatures that he describes himself as—'the most unteachable of all animals, their capacities never reaching higher than to draw or carry burthens.

Yet I am of the opinion this defect ariseth chiefly from a perverse, restive disposition. For they are cunning, malicious,
treacherous and revengeful. They are strong and hardy, but of a
cowardly spirit, and by consequence, insolent, abject, and
cruel.'

In *The English Humourists* Thackeray discusses this appalling
image of human nature, and in particular the episode of
Gulliver sheltering under a tree to avoid the rain of excrement
from the Yahoos:

'The reader of the fourth part of *Gulliver's Travels* is like the
hero himself in this instance. It is Yahoo language: a monster
gibbering shrieks, and gnashing imprecations against mankind
—tearing down all shreds of modesty, past all sense of manliness and shame; filthy in word, filthy in thought, furious,
raging, obscene.'

It is. After reading the Voyage to the Houyhnhnms it is
difficult not to see, at least for a while, humanity in the Yahoo
shape that Swift gave it, and like Gulliver to be sickened by the
smell and even the appearance of humankind. The description
of Gulliver's return, and his obsessional efforts to avoid contamination from the captain and crew of his rescue-ship, reads
like a psychoanalyst's case-history. 'The captain . . . offered to
lend me the best suit of clothes he had. This I would not be
prevailed upon to accept, abhorring to cover myself with anything that had been on the back of a Yahoo. I only desired he
would lend me two clean shirts, which having been washed
since he wore them, I believed would not so much defile
me . . .'

'. . . I remained silent and sullen; I was ready to faint at the
very smell of him and his men . . .'

'As soon as I entered the house, my wife took me in her arms,
and kissed me, at which, having not been used to the touch of
that odious animal for so many years, I fell in a swoon for
almost an hour. At the time I am writing it is five years since
my last return to England: during the first year I could not
endure my wife or children in my presence, the very smell of
them was intolerable, much less could I suffer them to eat in the
same room. To this hour they dare not presume to touch my
bread, or drink out of the same cup, neither was I ever able to let
one of them take me by the hand . . .'

'A frightful self-consciousness it must have been, which looked on mankind so darkly through those keen eyes of Swift,' says Thackeray. Perhaps if we were transported to the eighteenth century in England we might see it through Swift's eyes.

10. *Like a Diamond Begrimed with Dirt*

Two revolutions were going on in England at the end of the eighteenth century—two revolutions so intertwined that it is difficult to pick out the single strands, but both destined to make more changes in the life of the mass of English people than five hundred years of landowners' squabbles.

Mechanization was changing the face of every industry. As early as 1764 Hargreaves's first crude spinning jenny made it possible for one man to operate sixteen or eighteen spindles simultaneously—with the immediate effect that sixteen or eighteen times as much yarn could be produced per day, and also that men, whose arms were strong enough to move the clumsy mechanisms, came in out of the fields and began to replace women in the task of spinning. The improvements in machines followed tumbling one after another: Arkwright's spinning throstle in 1767, Crompton's mule in 1785, Arkwright's carding engine at about the same time (a necessary device to provide enough carded fibre to keep the spinning machines occupied) and Cartwright's power loom in 1804. The application of water-power or steam to all these machines made the factory system pre-eminent in the textile trade and virtually killed all home production of cloth except in the most remote districts. The tireless energy of steam, and the ability of machines to make endless repetitions of simple jobs, meant that as much material could be produced in a day as had taken two or more weeks for the hand spinners and weavers. As in the textile trade, so in every other industry, the machines multiplied output ten- or twenty-fold. Where the hands and arms of workers and craftsmen had just about sufficed to provide the bare necessities of life for the mass of Englishmen, the machines suddenly provided the means for giving everyone not only enough, but a superfluity, of every kind of necessity and luxury. They did not, of course, but that is another and darker story.

Many workmen began to see the machines and steam engines as malevolent and cunning monsters, stealing the bread out of men's mouths by force or trickery, and this image seems very apt when we consider the second revolution; the machines began to take over the land.

Work in the factories, and the possibility of escaping from harsh masters and back-breaking work on the farms, had attracted many agricultural workers to the towns, which were expanding at an unbelievable rate. Many small yeomen and smallholders followed suit, finding the prospects of regular wages more attractive than the hazards of failed harvests and diseased cattle. So the machines, like Sirens, lured men away from the land. At the same time, in the reassuring guise of Jethro Tull and the other agricultural machinery manufacturers, the machines crept round behind the departing farm-workers and began to take over the business of farming. Machines, and the success of the three-field system, made it attractive to farm large areas, instead of the mass of strips and smallholdings that had existed before, so landowners accelerated the process of change by enclosing common land, enlarging fields, and, inevitably, driving more farm-workers to the towns:

'There is one farmer, in the North of Hampshire, who has nearly eight thousand acres of land in his hands; who grows fourteen hundred acres of wheat and two thousand acres of barley! He occupies what was formerly 40 farms! Is it any wonder that paupers increase?' thundered Cobbett, but he was one man standing up to halt a procession of steam engines.

As a final blow to the old system, the Napoleonic Wars created a tremendous demand for food and supplies of all kinds. Manufacturers and farmers who had had the foresight to install the machines and embrace the new methods made fortunes: most of the others were driven to the wall. One lighter aspect of this fortune-making was that, in many cases for the first time, farmers and middle-class manufacturers had a lot of idle money to spend. The demand for luxuries, knick-knacks, articles of ostentation, suddenly widened from the old aristocracy to an entirely new class. Coleridge, rather unusually taking his eyes away from the study of German metaphysics to comment on life around him, referred to this change as 'the shoal of ostentatious fooleries and sensual vices which the sudden influx of wealth let in on our farmers and yeomanry', while Cobbett, always a lover of detail, describes the decline of a farmhouse in which the farmer's wife will no longer allow farm-workers to live because of her expensive furniture:

'Everything about this farmhouse was formerly the scene of *plain manners* and *plentiful living* . . . But all appeared to be in a state of decay and nearly of *disuse*. There appeared to have been hardly any *family* in that house, where formerly there were, in all probability, from ten to fifteen men, boys, and maids: and which was worst of all, there was a *parlour*. Aye, and a *carpet* and *bell-pull*, too!'

And higher up the social scale, worse than bell-pulls:

> The man is a shallow fool who cannot estimate the difference between . . . a resident *native* gentry, attached to the soil, known to every farmer and labourer from their child-hood, frequently mixing with them in those pursuits where all artificial distinctions are lost, practising hospitality without ceremony, from habit and not on calculation; and a gentry only now-and-then-residing at all, having no relish for country delights, foreign in their manners, distant and haughty in their behaviour, looking to the soil only for its rents, viewing it as a mere object of speculation, unacquainted with its cultivators, despising them and their pursuits, and relying for influence not upon the goodwill of the vicinage, but upon the dread of their power . . .

Paper-money and bank bills had also done their worst for England:

'The war and paper-system has brought in nabobs, Negro-drivers, governors, admirals, generals, loan-jobbers . . . con-tractors . . . pensioners . . . bankers . . . stockjobbers . . .'

All these objects of Cobbett's noisy dislike had one thing in common: their money insulated them from contact with the real sources of wealth. The landowners and large farmers were losing touch with the soil itself, and manufacturers and merchants were never called upon to handle the actual goods from which they drew their profits. But they all had money to spend and a show to make in the world, and to serve this new, rich, middle class with suitable objects for show, there was an enormous expansion in the number of shops, warehouses, importers and dealers. Each shopkeeper tried his utmost to become fashionable, influential, attracting new customers by the prestige of his existing ones, and many of them developed what we would now call 'sales gimmicks' to spread their fame abroad. One such gentleman was Nathaniel Bentley.

Thomas Bentley, his father, had been an enterprising young man who married into a moneyed family in his native town of Sudbury, Suffolk, became a merchant, and lived in some style with a pleasant house. He then took to religion, of a vaguely Methodist type, and in a curious fit of puritanism or calculation 'took the opportunity of his wife's absence to destroy all the pictures, the carpeting, and even the cornices of his best apartments; and finally to burn the best and gayest of her cloaths . . .' He then absconded to London and his wife seems (not surprisingly) to have stayed in Suffolk. Far from being mad, however, Thomas seems to have set himself up in another thriving business in Grafton Street, Soho, selling hardware, linens, and muslins, so perhaps his religion was truly Methodist.

Thomas left all his money to his son Nathaniel, who for some years lived the life of a rich young tradesman, running a warehouse in Leadenhall Street where he specialized in the sale of gold and silver goods, imported pottery, and other luxury articles. He appeared in society as something of a dandy, and had his hair dressed by a court perruquier.

As he approached his forties, however, a change became detectable, as if he had inherited features of his father's eccentricity. He employed only one man at the warehouse, despite his busy trade, and was often to be seen taking down and putting up his own shutters, dressed in dirty shirtsleeves and looking very different from his dandyish social figure. He still powdered his hair for going out, but it became increasingly obvious that the powder had not been applied by a court perruquier, and that it was spread over a thick layer of dust and dirt. When a friend mentioned the extreme dirtiness of his hands as he served a customer in the warehouse, he replied simply: 'It's of no use; if I wash my hands today, they will be dirty again tomorrow.'

The warehouse itself became drab and grimy, the windows almost opaque with dirt and cobwebs spread in every corner, and after a time Nathaniel came to be an object of editorial comment:

'This singular Phoenomenon lives at the house in Leadenhall-Street, known by the name of the DIRTY WAREHOUSE, situate at the corner of the passage leading to the house, originally the Old Crown Tavern . . .'

There were lampoons:

> . . . Persons there are, who say thou hast been seen
> (Some years ago) with hands and face wash'd clean;
> And wouldst though (*sic*) quit this most unseemly plan,
> Thou art ('tis said) a very comely man.
> Of polish'd language, partial to the fair,
> Then why not wash thy face, and comb thy matted hair;
> Clear from thy house accumulated dirt,
> New paint the front, and wear a cleaner shirt.*

Nathaniel paid no heed. When his business neighbours in Leadenhall Street remonstrated with him about the state of his premises and the bad effect that they had on the neighbourhood, he pointed out that it would be bad for his trade to alter the premises: 'from London to the Levant the house is best known by the name of the Dirty Warehouse of Leadenhall Street.' As to vermin, he often said that he would not have a dog or cat as company, because they destroyed one's property, and he had no rats or mice because he left them nothing to live on. Towards the end of his life he lived on eighteen pence a day, commenting: 'Anybody can that pleases. It is no hardship to me, though I used to have seven courses at dinner and three servants to wait on me.' On one occasion he invited some merchants to dinner, after a business transaction, much to their surprise, as his miserly habits were by now notorious. When they turned up in the dirty warehouse, Nathaniel, still in his dirty shirtsleeves, planked down on the grimy counter bread, a

* *European Magazine*, January 1801.

pound of cheese, and a jug of small ale, pointing out that the profits on their business would admit of no greater luxury.

From about 1805 he took to wandering abroad by himself every year, and when he died in 1809 it was in Musselburgh in Scotland. The warehouse was opened and found to be in a ruinous condition: the cooking utensils and plates were dilapidated and dirty, cobwebs, dust and dirt filled every corner, the steel grates were thick with rust, and the furniture, though once of good quality, was filled with dirt and insects.

The death of such an eccentric immediately brought comment from the pamphleteers and street ballad mongers. Pamphlets which had been prepared during his lifetime were reprinted (the two main sources are *The History of the Extraordinary Dirty Warehouse in Leadenhall Street, together with the Memoirs of its Eccentric Inhabitant Nath. Bentley Esq. To which are added the Memoirs of Mr. Thomas Bentley late of Sudbury, Never Before Published* (1803) and *Bentley's Life, the Only Genuine Edition, Authentic Memoirs of the Celebrated Nath. Bentley Esq.* (Commonly called *Dirty Dick*) *Late Proprietor of the Remarkable Dirty Warehouse No. 46 Leadenhall Street, Now carried on by Mr. Gosling* (1805)) and his life was discussed in the magazines. The incredible thing is the tone of reverence which is adopted towards such an obviously grasping and unpleasant old man:

'. . . we consider him as an *unique*, a kind of *non descript* in society. The cause, no doubt is a mixture of pride, a love of singularity, and a striking degree of avarice . . .'

It was said that he had 'considerable scholarly attainments, and could speak French and Italian fluently. Yet, in spite of his eccentricities, he was remarkably polite to ladies who, with the curiosity which is characteristic of all Eve's daughters, would often go to his shop, and were invariably pleased with the politeness of his manners.'

'He was like a diamond begrimed with dirt . . .'

In these passages we see the cunning of Bentley's public relations. It is difficult to imagine magazines praising any other shopkeeper for being polite to customers, or even praising an importer for knowing a little of some other language, yet because Bentley was dirty *and* polite, he attracted attention, and we know that customers still flocked to his shop. The wisdom or otherwise of his miserly and dirty habits is a matter of opinion, but there seems no doubt that a great deal of solid business calculation went into his 'eccentricity'.

The Victorians, of course, could not leave the story at that. Although there is no evidence for this in the contemporary accounts, Bentley was credited with a broken heart: according to this version, he was betrothed and had gone as far as preparing the wedding feast, when news came that his bride-to-be had died suddenly. He thereupon closed up the room with the feast and left the food to the mice and rats. In *Household Words* this tale is turned into a ballad:

> In a dirty old house lived a Dirty Old Man,
> Soap, towels or brushes were not in his plan;
> For forty long years as the neighbours declared,
> His house never once had been cleaned or repaired.
>
> 'Twas a scandal and shame to the business-like street,
> One terrible blot in a ledger so neat;
> The old shop with its glasses, black bottles and vats,
> And the rest of the mansion a run for the rats.
>
> Outside, the old plaster, all splatter and stain,
> Looked spotty in sunshine and streaky in rain;
> The window-sills sprouted with mildewy grass,
> And the panes being broken, were known to be glass.
>
> On a rickety signboard no learning could spell,
> The merchant who sold, or the goods he'd to sell;
> But for house and for man, a new title took growth,
> Like a fungus the dirt gave a name to them both.
>
> Within these were carpets and cushions of dust,
> The wood was half rot, and the metal half rust;
> Old curtains—half cobwebs—hung grimly aloof;
> 'Twas a spider's elysium from cellar to roof.
>
> There, king of the spiders, the Dirty old man,
> Lives busy, and dirty, as ever he can;
> With dirt on his fingers and dirt on his face,
> The Dirty Old Man thinks the dirt no disgrace . . .

and so on. The story told in *Household Words* is still told in the surviving 'Dirty Dick's' public house in Bishopsgate, which has a cellar full of grisly relics of the supposed wedding feast. It is, perhaps, a pity that the sentimental version has triumphed;

125

Nathaniel Bentley deserves to be remembered less for his sentiment than for his unique marketing campaign.

*

One of the consequences of the richer furnishings of the Regency and Victorian homes, among the middle-class, was the enormous increase in the numbers of bugs. Bed-bugs, *Cimex lectularius*, are retiring little creatures that do not like to be disturbed during the hours of daylight, and need plenty of warm cover in which to hide until they can creep out at night in search of their prey. Bugs have been in England since about the fifteenth century, and indeed the earlier versions of the Bible mention them. Where King James's Bible, in the Ninety-first Psalm, says: 'Thou shalt not be afraid for the terror by night; nor for the arrow that flieth by day,' Coverdale's Bible of 1535 has:

'Thou shalt not nede to be afrayed for any bugges by nights.'

Unlike Blake's 'invisible worm' they do not fly, but as they can run over any surface, even upside-down, this does not debar them from any bed where they are determined to join the human occupant:

'There are well authenticated records of people isolating their beds by means of saucers of paraffin placed under the legs so that the bugs could not climb up, and retiring to rest with a pleasant feeling of having foiled their enemies, only to be disturbed later in the night by bugs dropping from the ceiling.'*

Bugs are flat, oval, hairy insects about one-fifth of an inch long, usually mahogany brown in colour. They hide in cracks in plaster, woodwork, furniture or almost anywhere in a room near an occupied bed, and creep out very stealthily on to the human body. Their bite is not usually felt even by light sleepers, but they inject saliva in the same way that fleas do, and this saliva later sets up the characteristic irritation. They also have an unpleasant habit of turning round after feeding and defecating on the skin almost exactly over the bite, so that as soon as the sleeper begins to scratch germs are rubbed into the puncture: as bugs can carry relapsing fever germs this can be a serious matter. In any case, the itching from bug-bites is particularly intense, and

* *The Bed-Bug.* British Museum (Natural History) Econ. Series No. 5, 1949.

most sufferers tend to damage their skin and set up eruptions because of the frenzied scratching. The British Museum pamphlet cited above says that 'in infested areas it is often possible to pick out children from buggy homes by their pasty faces, listless appearance and general lack of energy ... sleepless nights with constant irritation due to the injection of minute doses of Bed-Bug saliva into the blood are likely to contribute largely to the ill-health of children and even of certain adults.'

In the nineteenth century bugs contributed to the discomfort, at least, of some very exalted adults. One of the more unusual Royal Appointments was to Tiffin and Son, *Bug-Destroyers to Her Majesty*: the senior partner of the firm gave a fascinating picture of the life of a Victorian bug-catcher when interviewed by Henry Mayhew, author of *London Labour and the London Poor*:

> ... I work for the upper classes only; that is, for carriage company and such-like approaching it, you know. I have noblemen's names, the first in England, on my books ... I was once at work on the Princess Charlotte's own bedstead. I was in the room, and she asked me if I had found anything, and I told her no; but just that minute I *did* happen to catch one, and upon that she sprang up on the bed, and put her hand on my shoulder, to look at it. She had been tormented by the creature, because I was ordered to come directly, and that was the only one I found. When the Princess saw it, she said 'Oh, the nasty thing! That's what tormented me last night; don't let him escape.' I think he looked all the better for having tasted royal blood.

Tiffin and Son were not the first to claim Royal Appointment for bug-catching: in 1775 there was an advertisement for 'Bug-Destroyer to His Majesty' which was hotly challenged by Andrew Cooke of Holborn Hill, who also claimed to have worked at the palace, and also to have 'cured 16,000 beds with great applause'. Mary Southall ('Successor to John Southall, the first and only person that ever found out the nature of BUGGS, Author of the Treatise of those nauseous venomous Insects, published with the Approbation ... of the Royal Society') not only acted as a bug-destroyer to quality and gentry, but also had the NON PAREIL LIQUOR on sale for those too poor to afford her personal services.

Tiffin's prejudice against iron bedsteads was not shared by most people: iron was usually considered a specific against bugs. However, the omniscient Miss Severn preferred scrubbing the floors with salt water:

"'But, Miss Anna, people have iron bedsteads now."

"'Iron will not prevent these troublesome pests from harbouring there, neither will what are termed brass bedsteads, unless they were made wholly of polished brass; there would be then no foot-hold for them. But in both iron and brass bedsteads, the latter having so much iron in them, I once saw these insects in numbers .. !"'*

Miss Severn does not use the word 'bugs', which had already passed out of polite usage by 1876. This reticence must have made life difficult for the professional bug-destroyers, and it did little to inhibit the proliferation of the insects themselves, as bugs were associated with bedrooms, particularly in lodging-houses, until DDT and lindane arrived to put an end to them.

Bugs, while they do not carry such serious diseases as lice or fleas, have the objectionable habit of emitting a nauseating smell as they are attacked. This is a special oil secreted in glands, which clings to surfaces and clothes for days: Balzac complained about the smell of bugs as the characteristic odour of French lodging-houses, and Orwell mentions them in *Down and Out in Paris and London* in 1933:

'The walls were as thin as matchwood, and to hide the cracks they had been covered with layer after layer of pink paper, which had come loose and housed innumerable bugs. Near the ceiling long lines of bugs marched all day like columns of soldiers, and at night came down ravenously hungry, so that one had to get up every few hours and kill them in hecatombs. Sometimes when the bugs got too bad one used to burn sulphur and drive them into the next room; whereupon the lodger next door would retort by having *his* room sulphured, and drive the bugs back. . . .'

And in Victorian times, back and forth they went, from the poorest hovel to the Princess Charlotte's bedstead. When the royal family and the aristocracy could not manage without the services of a bug-destroyer, it is impossible to conceive the number of bugs infesting the houses of the poor, all living up to

* *My Lady-Help, and What She Taught Me, Ladies' Treasury*, 1876.

the succinct description in Salmon's *New London Dispensatory* of 1702:

'*Cimex, Kopis, Apis*, The chinch, wall-louse, wood-louse, or buggs. Those that haunt beds are here meant: they are flat, red, and stinking, and suck man's blood greedily.'

11. Oh God! What I Saw!

To many people, and communities, there comes a time when difficulties pile up, one on another, until there seems no way even to start to unravel the mess. Social workers and the police are dismally familiar with the cases of neglect or cruelty to children that arise simply because the parents are unable to cope with life. Perhaps one of the children falls ill, and there is no one to look after the others, so either the sick or the well have to be neglected for a time. The house gets dirty and food goes bad, the children's clothes get ragged and soiled, and these things in themselves add to the problems: the mother would welcome help, but dare not ask anyone into the house in its filthy state . . . and so the vicious circle continues.

'It's been going on for three months,' said one mother, desperately. 'I don't seem to be able to manage anything. I know I could get a sitter for the children, but I'm ashamed to let anyone in. . . .'

The same reaction tends to set in when there is a disaster—a flood, a fire, an earthquake. All the services are cut off, food is short, water is infected, and the most dreadful thing is that no one knows where to begin to put things back to normal. Often a terrible apathy sets in. Rescue teams know that their hardest task is sometimes to induce the stricken community to help itself.

For a family in this situation, there are social workers and neighbours: for a small community there are rescue teams, the Red Cross, doctors and nurses. But what if the stricken community is the whole of a nation, and there is no outside help?

Victorian England leaves one with this impression; a nation in a state of disaster, with such enormous and terrifying problems in its social system that no one knew where to start to solve them.

The Industrial Revolution was at its height. Factories were rising like ant-hills over the face of England, and workers were swarming into the towns away from the impoverished country-side. Houses had to be found for them, and found fast.

'. . . . an individual who may have a couple of thousand pounds does not exactly know what to do with it, having no occasion for it in trade; he wishes to lay it out so as to pay him the best percentage in money; he will purchase a plot of ground, an acre or half an acre; then what he thinks about is, to place as many houses on this acre of ground as he possibly can, without reference to drainage or anything, except that which will pay him a good percentage for his money; that is the way in which the principal part of the suburbs of Bradford has sprung up.'*

Bradford grew from a town of 29,000 people in 1801 to 77,000 in 1831, so 48,000 people were housed in these jerry-built hovels thrown up by gentlemen with 'a couple of thousand pounds' to spare. Leeds, in the same years, increased from 53,000 to 123,000: London added almost 200,000 to her teeming population in the years 1815 to 1820 alone. Houses were rushed on to the available open spaces, filling up the squares, backing on to other rows of houses, piled up crazily in tenements. They took every available space like stalls filling up a market square on a fair day, and were often no more substantial:

'The walls are only half brick thick, or what the bricklayers call "brick noggin", and the whole of the materials are slight and unfit for the purpose . . . they are built back to back; without ventilation or drainage; and, like a honeycomb, every particle of space is occupied. Double rows of these houses form courts, with, perhaps, a pump at one end and a privy at the other, common to the inhabitants of about twenty houses.'†

* *Report of the Health of Towns Committee*, 1840.
† From the same Report.

In St. Giles, London, a whole large square was gradually filled with rows of houses, starting at the circumference and building inwards until there was an almost solid maze or 'rookery' like a set of Chinese boxes. In all this enormous mass of habitation there was no drainage, no sewers, water pumps only at rare intervals, and no lighting. Engels describes the district in that great, compassionate book, *The Condition of the Working Class in England in 1844*, after tramping round its filthy courts:

It is a disorderly collection of tall, three- or four-storied houses, with narrow, crooked, filthy streets, in which there is quite as much life as in the great thoroughfares of the town, except that, here, people of the working class only are to be seen. A vegetable market is held in the street, baskets with vegetables and fruits, naturally all bad and hardly fit to use, obstruct the sidewalk still further, and from these, as well as from the fish-dealers' stalls, arises a horrible smell. The houses are occupied from cellar to garret, filthy within and without, and their appearance is such that no human being could possibly wish to live in them. But all this is nothing in comparison with the dwellings in the narrow courts and alleys between the streets, entered by covered passages between the houses, in which the filth and tottering ruin surpass all description. Scarcely a whole window-pane can be found, the walls are crumbling, doorposts and window-frames loose and broken, doors of old boards nailed together, or altogether wanting in this thieves' quarter, where no doors are needed, there being nothing to steal. Heaps of garbage and ashes lie in all directions, and the foul liquids emptied before the doors gather in stinking pools. Here live the poorest of the poor, the worst paid workers with thieves and the victims of prostitution indiscriminately huddled together, the majority Irish, or of Irish extraction, and those who have not yet sunk in the whirlpool of moral ruin which surrounds them, sinking daily deeper, losing daily more and more of their power to resist the demoralizing influence of want, filth, and evil surroundings.

In the Edinburgh wynds, according to *The Artisan* for October 1843:

These streets are often so narrow that a person can step from the window of one house into that of its opposite neighbour, while the houses are piled so high, storey upon storey, that the light can scarcely penetrate into the court or alley that lies between. In this part of the city there are neither sewers nor other drains, nor even privies belonging to the houses. In consequence, all refuse, garbage, and excrements of at least 50,000 persons are thrown into the gutters every night, so that, in spite of all street sweeping, a mass of dried filth and foul vapours are created, which not only offend the sight and smell, but endanger the health of the inhabitants in the highest degree.

This is a rather different picture of Edinburgh than that conjured up by the pious hopes of the *Regulations to be Attended to by Domestic Servants and others* under the Edinburgh Police Act of 1848:

. . . That every offensive matter or thing shall be taken in pails or buckets, or other proper vessels, to the streets or courts, to be emptied into the dust-carts, by the Scavengers and Carters, under a penalty not exceeding 40s for each offence . . .

. . . That if any person shall throw or cast from any window or other place any water, dung, soil, dirt, ashes or filth, or any offensive matter or thing, into or upon any street or court, back ground, garden, or place, he shall . . . be liable to a penalty not exceeding 40s . . .

. . . If any person shall throw upon any street or court any dung, soil, dirt, ashes or filth, or shall discharge upon any street or court, by means of any soil or foul-water pipe, any dung, soil, dirt, or filth, or shall accumulate within any enclosure, area, dwelling-house, garret, cellar or other apartment, any dung, soil, dirt, ashes or filth. . . .

One is inclined to believe the description, not the regulations, gives the true picture of Edinburgh in the 1840s: Edinburgh is still a remarkably filthy city, and one of the few large cities left in Great Britain which still discharges 'dung, soil, dirt, and filth' into near-by waterways. It often seems that the Athens of the North could adopt 'Gardy Loo!' as its civic motto.

The Scottish towns, despite their smaller populations, seem to have been unusually nauseating. In Greenock, Dr. Laurie commented in 1842:

> In one part of Market Street is a dunghill—yet it is too large to be called a dunghill. I do not misstate its size when I say it contains a hundred cubic yards of impure filth, collected from all parts of the town. It is never removed; it is the stock-in-trade of a person who deals in dung; he retails it by cartfuls. To please his customers, he always keeps a nucleus, as the older the filth is the higher the price. The proprietor has an extensive privy attached to the concern. This collection is fronting the public street; it is enclosed in front by a wall; the height of the wall is almost twelve feet, and the dung overtops it; the malarious moisture oozes through the wall, and runs over the pavement.
>
> The effluvia all round this place in summer is horrible. There is a land of houses adjoining, four stories in height, and in the summer each house swarms with myriads of flies; every article of food and drink must be covered, otherwise, if left exposed for a minute, the flies immediately attack it, and it is rendered unfit for use, from the strong taste of the dunghill left by the flies.

Inside the houses, conditions were as bad as outside. In 1843, at an inquest on Ann Galway, aged forty-five years, found dead at No. 3 White Lion Court, Bermondsey Street, London, the coroner was told that the body had been found in the one room shared by Ann, her husband, and their nineteen-year-old son. There was no furniture, not even a bed, but they slept on a pile of dirty feathers, which had stuck so firmly to her almost naked body that the surgeon had to have the body washed before he could conduct the post-mortem. She was starving and covered with the pocks of flea and bug bites. Part of the floor had been torn up, the planks used for a fire and the hole was used by the family as a privy.

And these were *homes*. The number of homeless was so great that we have the incredible situation of Engels, the communist, stating the position with icy precision, 'In London fifty thousand human beings get up every morning, not knowing where they are to lay their heads at night', while *The Times* flew into a passion of radical rhetoric:

> It is indeed a monstrous state of things! Enjoyment the most absolute, that bodily ease, intellectual excitement, or the more innocent pleasures of sense can supply to man's craving, brought in close contact with the most unmitigated misery! Wealth, from its bright saloons, laughing—an insolently heedless laugh—at the unknown wounds of want! Pleasure, cruelly but unconsciously mocking the pain that moans below! . . .
>
> But let all men remember this—that within the most courtly precincts of the richest city of God's earth, there may be found, night after night, winter after winter, women— young in years—old in sin and suffering—outcasts from society—*Rotting from famine, filth, and disease.* Let them remember this, and learn not to theorize but to act. God knows, there is much room for action nowadays.*

The Top People of 1843 tut-tutted, or gave a shilling to a soup-kitchen, or wrote to *The Times.* Nothing was done to make more houses available, or to improve the conditions of those already there.

One of the greatest privations, and one which led to most of the dirt and unpleasantness, was the sheer lack of water. Most people had to carry water from pumps that might be several streets away, or from standpipes that were only turned on intermittently. Chadwick, the great reformer of our public health system, wrote about the difficulties of the working family:

> The whole family of the labouring man in the manufacturing towns rise early, before daylight in winter-time, to go to their work; they toil hard, and they return to their homes late at night. It is a serious inconvenience, as well as discomfort, to them to have to fetch water at a distance out of doors from the pump, or the river, on every occasion that it may be wanted, whether it may be in cold, in rain, or in snow. The minor comforts of cleanliness are, of course, forgone, to avoid the immediate and greater discomforts of having to fetch the

* 12 October, 1843.

water. . . . It is only when the infant enters upon breathing existence, and when the man has ceased to breathe—at the moment of birth and at the hour of death—that he is really well washed.

Even in the really dirty trades, washing was not always considered necessary, either by the employers or the workers themselves.

'*Peter Gaskell*, a collier in the Worsley pits, Lancashire, when asked, "How often do the drawers wash their bodies?" replied, "None of the drawers does wash their bodies; I never wash my body; I let my shirt rub the dirt off, my shirt will show that; I wash my neck and ears and face, of course."' This was evidence offered during an enquiry which led to the Coal Mines Regulation Act of 1842. Colliers had a traditional belief that water was weakening, and even in this century avoided soaking their backs in hot water, but one can imagine the shirt that had rubbed the dirt off a drawer, a man engaged in manhandling coal tubs to the pit shaft. Women and children also did this work: the same collier—'. . . to the further question, "Do you think it is usual for the young women to do the same as you do?" he replied, "I don't think it is usual for the lasses to wash their bodies; my sisters never wash themselves, and seeing is believing; they wash their faces and necks and ears."'

One of these poor wretches, Ann Eggley, 18-year-old hurrier in Messrs Thorpe's colliery, sums up in her few artless words the whole squalid disaster of the Industrial Revolution and its effects on the working-class:

I'm sure I don't know how to spell my name. We go at four in the morning and sometimes at half-past four. We begin to work as soon as we get down. We get out after four, sometimes at five, in the evening. I hurry by myself, and have done so for long.

I know the corves are very heavy, they are the biggest corves anywhere about. The work is far too hard for me; the sweat runs off me all over sometimes. I am very tired at night. Sometimes when we get home at night we have not the power to wash us, and then we go to bed. Sometimes we fall asleep in the chair.

Father said last night it was both a shame and a disgrace

for girls to work as we do, but there is naught else for us to do . . .*

Where they did manage to wash, the women were unlikely to have any privacy in the crowded houses, and mostly adopted an attitude of indifference to modesty, which was inevitable in the circumstances, but greatly shocked the Victorian investigators: Edward Newman, solicitor of Barnsley, reported on the mining community:

'At Silkstone there are a great many girls who work in the pits, and I have seen them washing themselves naked much below the waist as I passed their doors, and whilst they are doing this, they will be talking and chatting with any man who happen to be there with the utmost unconcern, and men young and old would be washing in the same place, at the same time . . .'

Some families depended upon the water-carriers who plied the streets. In Bradford and Chorlton-on-Medlock the charge was 1d. for three gallons, in Carlisle 1d for eight gallons—but wages were rarely more than fourteen shillings a week.

The standpipes or pumps were not available all the time. Often they were running for only a few minutes per day in the poorer districts, and this caused fights and struggles to get the precious liquid before the supply failed: 'I have seen as many as from 20 to 50 persons with pails waiting round one or two stand-pipes. Then there is quarrelling for the turn; the strongest pushing forward, and the pails, after they are filled, being upset.' In Snows Rents in Westminster there was a near-riot when the one pipe that supplied sixteen houses was turned on for only five minutes one Sunday, despite the fact that Sunday was the favoured (and, for the working wife, the only) washing day. Yet the Reverend Whitwell Elwin, Chaplain to the Bath Union, could say smugly: 'With the poor, far less obstacles are an absolute barrier (*to cleanliness*), because no privation is felt by them so little as that of cleanliness. The propensity to dirt is so strong, the steps so few and easy, that nothing but the utmost facilities for water can act as a counterpoise; and such is the love of uncleanliness, when once contracted, that no habit, not even drunkenness, is so difficult to eradicate.' The reverend gentleman meant well: he was trying to persuade the Bath

* Parliamentary Papers, 1842.

authorities to spare a little water for the needy, but the tone of patronage took little heed of the desperate struggles of many poor housewives to keep their families clean. In Leeds there were complaints that the washing lines made the streets dangerous for horsemen.

Some pioneers were successful. In Liverpool an Irish immigrant, Mrs. Kitty Wilkinson, belied all the tales of the filth of the Irish by setting up a public wash-house in her kitchen during an epidemic, enabling her neighbours to boil and clean their linen, and preventing a great deal of infection. William Rathbone did the far more remarkable thing of making the Liverpool Corporation see that Mrs. Wilkinson's enterprise could be extended by the municipality, and in 1842 Liverpool had baths and wash-houses where anyone could obtain a warm bath for 2d., a cold bath for 1d., and the use of a tub and hot water for washing clothes for 1d. Kitty Wilkinson is commemorated in a window in Liverpool Anglican Cathedral.

But the water was becoming hard to get—at least in any decent state to drink. At the end of *Oliver Twist* Dickens describes the inhabitants of houses near Jacob's Island getting their water from Folly Ditch, a muddy backwater of the Thames:

> At such times, a stranger looking from one of the wooden bridges thrown across it at Mill Lane, will see the inhabitants of the houses on either side lowering from their back doors and windows, buckets, pails, domestic utensils of all kinds, in which to haul the water up; and when his eye is turned from these operations to the houses themselves, his utmost astonishment will be excited by the scene before him. Crazy wooden galleries common to the backs of half a dozen houses, with holes from which to look out upon the slime beneath; windows, broken and patched, with poles thrust out, on which to dry the linen that is never there; rooms so small, so filthy, so confined, that the air would seem too tainted even for the dirt and squalor which they shelter; wooden chambers thrusting themselves out above the mud, and threatening to fall into it—as some have done; dirt-besmeared walls and decaying foundations; every repulsive lineament of poverty, every loathsome indication of filth, rot, and garbage; all these ornament the banks of Folly Ditch.

It is unpleasant to imagine what it was that their buckets and pails brought up. The Thames was foul beyond belief: still slow-moving because of the large number of mill-weirs and dams, it now carried the untreated sewage from about 10,000 Bramah closets and a tremendous amount of private enterprise. In the industrial north, the rivers were already becoming contaminated by chemical wastes and the outpourings of steam engines; in Leeds, for instance:

'The Aire . . . like all other rivers in the service of manufacture, flows into the city at one end clear and transparent, and flows out at the other end thick, black, and foul, smelling of all possible refuse . . .'

This was Engels on the subject of Leeds: about Manchester, of which he could fairly say that he knew the town better than many of its natives, he commented:

'The Irk, a narrow, coal-black, foul-smelling stream, full of debris and refuse, which it deposits on the shallower right bank. In dry weather, a long stream of the most disgusting, blackish-green, slime pools are left standing on this bank, from the depths of which bubbles of miasmatic gas constantly arise and give forth a stench unendurable even on the bridge forty or fifty feet above the surface of the stream.' The Irwell was similar.

These rivers provided the drinking water. For those who were too far from the river to collect even the polluted water which they contained, and who had no pump or standpipe, water had to come out of the gutters.

J. Riddall Wood, in another enquiry, gave evidence about the 'water supply' of Liverpool:

'There is one circumstance which very much affects the atmosphere in these districts in which the cellars are particularly; there is a great deal of broken ground, in which there are pits; the water accumulates in those pits, and of course at the fall of the year there is a great deal of water in them, in which there have been thrown dead dogs and cats, and a great many offensive articles. The water is nevertheless used for culinary purposes. I could not believe this at first. I thought it was used only for washing, but I found it was used by the poorer inhabitants for culinary purposes.'

In Bradford, James Smith reported:

'The chief sewerage, if sewerage it can be called, of the

inferior streets and of the courts, is in open channels, and from the rough and unequal surface of the streets, the flow is tardy and the whole soil is saturated with sewage water. The main sewers are discharged either into the brook or into the terminus or basin of a canal that runs into the lower part of the town. The water of this basin is often so charged with decaying matter, that in hot weather bubbles of sulphureted hydrogen are continually rising to the surface, and so much is the atmosphere loaded with that gas, that watch cases and other materials of silver become black . . .' The brook and canal provided the water supply for the area.

'I was yesterday,' wrote Charles Kingsley to his sister, '. . . over the cholera districts of Bermondsey, and, oh God! What I saw! People having no water to drink—hundreds of them—but the water of the common sewer which stagnates, full of . . . dead fish, cats and dogs, under their windows.'

Cholera had come from India: the worst epidemic started in Jessore, about seventy miles from Calcutta, in 1817, and spread with terrifying speed through British India and beyond to Europe. The *cholera vibrio* found the European cities hospitable places in which to multiply—they were all as filthy as the large British towns, although at that time not quite as polluted with industrial waste—and the crowded, sewage-filled streets of London and the industrial north of England provided nutrient media, as the bacteriologists say, of exceptional value for the little comma-shaped creatures.

The disease is a particularly violent form of dysentery. The first symptoms are usually a sensation of giddiness, accompanied by ringing in the ears, and a general feeling of anxiety and uneasiness in the stomach. According to a pamphlet issued by the Board of Health in 1831, the next symptoms are—'a prodigious evacuation, when the whole intestines seem to be emptied at once . . . If the attack occurs in the day, the patient sits down affrighted at his own situation; or if in bed awakes and lies for a moment astonished at the novelty of his feelings; there is a new influence that appears to pervade the whole of his body, a sensation as if of fluttering in the pit of the stomach, and a sense of weight or constriction round the waist. This is followed by a prickly sensation in the arms and legs, extending sometimes to the fingers and toes; the hands and feet become bedewed

with a copious clammy moisture; the pulse is generally sup-
pressed and slow . . . and there is often a pain in the forehead.
The moment the patient moves . . . he is either sick or purged.
This lasts from half an hour to an hour, in pretty rapid succession.'

The diarrhoea and vomiting carried on until the patient had
no more fluid in his body to expel. The intestines produced
pints of cloudy liquid, with tiny white fragments in them, called
in the medical textbooks 'rice-water motions' but actually consisting of tiny fragments of the wall of the intestines flaking
away. The body became dehydrated, and often the doctors
would find the bed saturated with liquid and the floor of the
room awash, while the patient was wizened and dried up to the
appearance of a monkey, not a man. We cannot conceive what
such a disease must have been like in those tiny rooms, with no
privy, no drainage, no privacy: to lie there, fully conscious (for
cholera does not soften the blow even by delirium or uncon-
sciousness, except right at the end), feeling one's body dissolving
away into filth, like Poe's M. Valdemar.

After the loss of liquid, the cramps began. These were intense
pains, first in the fingers and toes, then up the limbs and across
the chest. The sufferers threw themselves about in their sodden
beds, and the skin turned blue or black. The pains were
intense: 'like being screwed through with a screw' or like
'having a sword put in on one side of the waist, just above the
hip-bone, and drawn through, handle and all . . .' Very often
the patients went into convulsions and rolled into a ball which
could not be straightened out after death. Most patients who
passed through this stage went into collapse and died from two
to three hours up to a week later.

The *cholera vibrio* is carried in contaminated water, and this
made cholera a disease peculiar to the poor. In many places
there were dire rumours that landowners, nobility, or others had
deliberately poisoned the mass of the people, and in Russia in
July 1831 a mob rioted in the streets of St. Petersburg to protest
against being 'poisoned' by the rich. They broke into a hospital
and 'rescued' the cholera patients, and were only turned away
from further violence when the Czar himself came into the street
and fell on his knees in prayer, that the plague should not be
spread further by his subjects' folly. In true Russian fashion, the

rioters burst into tears and joined him on their knees. More sophisticated peasants and workers, influenced by the view of Malthus (his *Essay on Population* had been published in 1798, and was well known throughout Europe), suspected that cholera was part of a campaign by the ruling classes to reduce the population. In Hungary, where 100,000 people died of cholera in 1831, the mobs tortured servants of the nobility, whom they had captured, until they 'confessed' that the disease had been deliberately spread by their masters.

This was madness enough, but the madness which struck in this country was a particularly English one. To state it in cold terms is to make it sound incredible, but—the English, finding that cholera epidemics restricted their freedom of movement and trade, solemnly denied that there was any such disease as cholera at all.

William Sproat was a sixty-year-old keelman, bringing coal on barges from up the river near Sunderland, and loading it on to deep-sea ships in the harbour. He lived in a large, well-ventilated room on the first floor of a house in Fish Quay, Sunderland, overlooking the harbour where he worked. On Wednesday 19 October, 1831, he was forced to stay away from work with diarrhoea, and on Thursday he felt ill enough to send for a doctor, a surgeon called Holmes. 'I found him vomiting and purging,' said Mr. Holmes. On Friday he felt a little better, and actually went to visit his barge on the Saturday, but was immediately taken with cramps. His friends called Mr. Holmes again, and, on the Sunday morning, 'I found him evidently sinking; pulse almost imperceptible and extremities cold, skin dry, eyes sunk, lips blue, features shrunk, he spoke in whispers, violent vomiting and purging, cramps of the calves of the legs and complete prostration of strength.'

It was a textbook case of cholera, and Mr. Holmes, who had not seen the disease before, felt sufficiently sure of his book-learning to report it as a case of cholera to Dr. Reid Clanny, a member of the Sunderland Board of Health, and to Dr. James Butler Kell, an army doctor stationed in the local barracks with the 82nd Reserve Regiment, and one of the few doctors in England who had actually seen cholera at first hand, during his Indian service. They both agreed with Holmes's diagnosis and helped him care for the patient—all in vain, however, for

William Sproat died in a coma on 26 October, the first official cholera victim in England. His granddaughter, a child of eleven, began to show the unmistakable symptoms about an hour after her grandfather's death, and his son William, 'a fine athletic young man', developed them on the Thursday.

Convinced that he was seeing the beginnings of a cholera epidemic, and knowing from experience the appalling speed with which the disease could spread, Kell reported the cases to the chairman of the Board of Health and asked him to contact the Government in London. There was argument about this step, for several local doctors considered that the attacks were nothing more than 'normal' dysentery, but after William Sproat junior had died, and a nurse at the Infirmary who had attended him, and two other people apparently not connected with the Sproat family, Dr. Clanny obtained agreement that cholera had arrived in Sunderland, and sent off a report to the Central Board of Health in London. Two half-pay officers with experience of cholera in India were immediately sent to Sunderland to report on the position and give all the assistance they could to the local doctors. Lieut.-Colonel Creagh, one of the experts from London, exercised his authority and imposed a fifteen-day quarantine on all shipping leaving Sunderland on November.

This act brought down a storm of protest from the shipowners and merchants:

'. . . the merchants, shipowners and inhabitants, who suffer from the restraints imposed upon an infected place, are loudly complaining of the measures which have been adopted, and strenuously insisting that their town is in a more healthy state than usual . . .' wrote Charles Greville in his diary for 14 November. The Marquis of Londonderry, who had married the local coalfield, felt even more strongly about this interference with his family life, and wrote to the London *Standard*, from the House of Lords, that the alarm was false.

A diagnosis from such impeccable sources could not be contradicted, and on 12 November, a day or two after his Lordship's letter had been published, an assembly of most of the doctors in Sunderland solemnly declared that '. . . as to the nature of the disorder which had created unnecessarily so great an excitement in the public mind, the same is not the Indian

Cholera, nor of foreign origin'. It added, with a vicious side-
swipe at Dr. Kell: '. . . the paragraph inserted in the London
newspapers . . . wherein it is stated that the Asiatic or conti-
nental cholera had been introduced into this town, by shipping
from Hamburg, is a most wicked and malicious falsehood . . .'
Kell, in fact, found himself as much an 'enemy of the people' as
Ibsen's hero, and was persuaded not to attend public meetings
because of the danger of physical attack from his opponents,
who constituted most of the business men and public figures of
the town. By blatant railroading, they gained control of the
Board of Health, and forbade Dr. Clanny to continue with his
practice of publishing lists of 'cholera' cases in the local newspapers—to his credit, he continued to do so at his own expense,
for there was a steady stream of deaths.

By this time, the contest between the coal industry and truth
was becoming too abominable for even the robust subjects of
William IV. Greville commented on the situation as seen from
London:

> When Dr. Russell was in Russia he was disgusted with the
> violence and prejudices he found there on the part of both
> medical men and the people, and he says he finds just as
> much here. The conduct of the people of Sunderland on this
> occasion is more suitable to the barbarism of the interior of
> Africa than to a town in a civilized country. The medical men
> and the higher classes split into parties, quarrelling about the
> nature of the disease, and perverting and concealing facts
> which militate against their respective theories. The people
> are taught to believe that there is really no cholera at all, and
> that those who say so intend to plunder and murder them.
> The consequence is prodigious irritation and excitement, an
> invincible repugnance on the part of the lower orders to
> avail themselves of any of the preparations which are made
> for curing them, and a proneness to believe any reports,
> however monstrous and exaggerated. In a very curious letter
> which was received yesterday from Dr. Daur [one of the
> London experts sent by the Central Board of Health] he says
> (after complaining of the medical men, who would send him
> no returns of the cases of sickness) it was believed that bodies
> had been dissected before the life was out of them, and one

woman was said to have been cut up while she was begging to be spared.

Some of these stories no doubt arose because of the rather heartless scientific curiosity displayed by many visitors to Sunderland. Cholera was almost unknown in many parts of Europe, and entirely unknown in the rest of the British Isles, and many doctors travelled to the town to study the disease at first hand. The sufferers must often have thought themselves in a delirium of fever to find a crowd of strangers, often speaking strange tongues, massing round them and subjecting them to the rather barbarous medical 'science' of the day. Fortunately one of the visitors was Dr. David Barry, a high-powered expert on cholera who had studied the epidemic in Russia earlier in the year, and arrived in Sunderland with full powers vested in him by the Central Board of Health. Dr. Barry was in no doubt that the disease, which was by now ravaging the town, was Asiatic cholera, and he reported this to London on 23 November. His report stirred the tender-hearted Greville to a comment that must have been true of many people in his position:

'He describes some cases he had visited, exhibiting scenes of misery and poverty far exceeding what one could have believed it possible to find in this country; but we who float on the surface of society know but little of the privations and suffering which pervade the mass . . .' Although to be fair to Greville, he had shown a rather acute knowledge of conditions in Sunderland at the beginning of the outbreak, for he wrote on 14 November:

The reports from Sunderland exhibit a state of human misery, and necessarily of moral degradation, such as I hardly ever heard of, and it is no wonder, when a great part of the community is plunged into such a condition . . . that there should be so many who are ripe for any desperate scheme of revolution. At Sunderland they say there are houses with 150 inmates, who are huddled five and six in a bed. They are in the lowest state of poverty. The sick in these receptacles are attended by an apothecary's boy, who brings them (or I suppose tosses them) medicines without distinction or enquiry.

Stirrings of conscience occurred in the most surprising hearts: the *Lancet* was moved, on 4 February 1832, to abandon its detached medical approach, and venture on social comment about 'the subordination of medical opinion, and the recklessness and avarice of a knot of mercantile speculators. . . . What now must be the feelings of the men—convicted either of gross and unexampled ignorance, or of equally shameful venality—who, with bared faces, erect and conspicuous before the world, continued to deny the existence of an unusual disease, until the choked graveyards of their town bore witness to the deplorable fact . . .'

The deplorable fact, having decimated Sunderland, spread to Gateshead, Newcastle, Edinburgh, Glasgow . . . down to London, across to the west country, causing great ravages in Exeter, and through the industrial north to Manchester. It struck in south Wales, particularly in the mining districts, where the wet conditions and complete lack of sanitation made miners an easy target: the disease spread down the pit and was then broadcast from home to home as the infected miners went through the stages of diarrhoea and vomiting.

Treatments were varied and usually as dangerous as the disease. Pitch plasters spread on the stomach, the fumes of muriatic (hydrochloric) acid and nitric acid, burning tar, turpentine, vinegar, flashing gunpowder, and camphor spirits 'thrown about the apartment' were some recipes. Dr. A. B. Granville, with some lack of thought, one feels, about the circumstances of most of the cholera sufferers, recommended oysters, partridge, pheasant and grouse. Chloride of lime, recommended for disinfecting everything in the house and on the body, would have been effective to some extent, but it was probably not used where it was most needed—in the drinking water. On the basis that warmth was essential, one ingenious individual invented a machine for passing warm air under the bedclothes. In his first experiment he set fire to the bed: in the second the gas used to provide the heat somehow failed to ignite until it had been passing into the bedclothes for several minutes . . . at least that patient did not die of cholera. If we could believe the figures published, the most successful treatment was devised by the President of the Board of Health in Ipswich, who presented the following simple table:

	Cases	Deaths
Treated with calomel and opium	9	5
Treated with emetics	2	2
Treated according to the plan advised in my treatise on cholera	12	0

The method was a suppository of soap and opium. Treatment with emetics in a disease where vomiting is a symptom may seem strange logic, but there was still a great residue of Paracelsus-type thinking in medicine (indeed, there is today: medicine is still less of a science than a kind of Russian roulette with drugs for bullets), and the idea of the 'counter-irritant' died hard. So did the patients. Some doctors, reluctant to give up the practice of bleeding that had been the mainstay of medicine for a century, but realizing vaguely that cholera patients could not very well spare any more fluid than they had already lost, adopted the course of pouring saline fluid into one arm while bleeding the other. Opium was undoubtedly the kindest of the treatments, and it did something to soothe the agonizing griping of the bowels, which tended to go on trying to expel fluid when the poor patient had no more to lose. One can have only sympathy for the Widow Proudfoot, mentioned in the *Glasgow Medical Journal* for 1832: '. . . an old, debilitated, intemperate woman, was seized and died early next morning, having refused any medicine except whisky.'

Otherwise there were cholera lozenges, cholera candy, cholera snuff and a host of other remedies, nearly all based on opium. Laudanum, a tincture of opium, was still the favourite analgesic in those days before aspirin and codeine: it combined pain-killing properties with a useful soothing effect on the digestive system, very necessary when starvation and coarse food were the lot of most of the poor. Old traditions of folk medicine still flourished, and many poor families added to their dangers of infection by heaping manure under their windows or sitting over a privy breathing in the fumes—just as their ancestors had done during the Black Death.

None of these remedies halted the infection, or prevented the second and third epidemics in 1848–9 and 1853–4. What finally gave man victory over the cholera *vibrio* was the realization, and effective proof, by Dr. John Snow, that cholera was spread by contamination of drinking water by sewage. His pamphlet 'On the mode of communication of cholera' (1849) and his book of the same name (1855) explained all the worst outbreaks: carefully drawn maps showed the number of cholera cases around each contaminated well or stream, and statistics connected the heaviest mortality with the poorest sanitary conditions.

Charles Kingsley warmly supported Snow's theory and put it to dramatic use in his novel *Two Years Ago*, which appeared in 1856 and dealt with a cholera epidemic in a small village. Kingsley produced a best-seller and made a great deal of money: Snow was left £200 out of pocket for the costs of producing his life-saving book.

The deaths from cholera in London alone—14,000 in the 1848–9 outbreak—seemed to do little to stir Parliament to action: the event that brought the conditions of London's water home to the members was a less tragic one. In the summer of 1858 there was a combination of unprecedented sun and very low rainfall. The Thames and other rivers began to shrink visibly as water became more and more short, the river bed began to appear exposed to the sun at all states of the tide, and many sewer outlets which had been concealed safely under the water level were left open to the air. The combined effects of concentrated sewage and sun produced an effluvium over the bed of the Thames that was remarkable even for Victorian times. During 'The Great Stink' it was suggested that Parliament had better be moved out of London, or at least a long way from the river: during the debate it was necessary to hang wet cloths soaked in chloride of lime over all the windows and doors in an attempt to neutralize the smell, but even this had very little success, and the debate dissolved in disorder. It may only be coincidence, but if there is any date from which one could clearly see a real effort to improve the sewerage systems of the country, it is 1858. About this time the sewers were surveyed officially, and Mayhew reported on the extraordinary results which emerged:

> . . . a sewer from the Westminster Workhouse, which was of all shapes and sizes, was in so wretched a condition that the leveller could scarcely work for the thick scum that covered the glasses of the spirit-level in a few minutes after being

wiped . . . a chamber is reached about 30 feet in length, from the roof of which hangings of putrid matter like stalactities descend three feet in length. At the end of this chamber, the sewer passes under the public privies, the ceilings of which can be seen from it. Beyond this it is not possible to go. . . .

The deposit has been found to comprise all the ingredients from the breweries, the gas-works, and the several chemical and mineral manufactories; dead dogs, cats, kittens and rats; offal from slaughter-houses, sometimes even including the entrails of the animals; street-pavement dirt of every variety; vegetable refuse; stable-dung; the refuse of pig-styes; night-soil; ashes; tin-kettles and pans (panshreds); broken stoneware, as jars, pitchers, flower-pots &c.; bricks, pieces of wood; rotten mortar and rubbish of different kinds; and even rags. . . .

On the 12th January we were very nearly losing a whole party by choke damp, the last man being dragged out on his back (through two feet of black foetid deposits) in a state of insensibility . . .

There is so much rottenness and decay that there is no security for the sewers standing from day to day, and to flush them for the removal of their 'most loathsome deposits' might be 'to bring some of them down altogether'.

If the waters in and under Victorian towns caused their own problems, the air was little better. Atmospheric pollution in the nineteenth century reached levels which have never been surpassed in this country, and could only be matched by some of the industrial towns in the USA. Coal production, to feed the ever-hungry machines, was rising sharply: 16 million tons in 1815, 30 million in 1835, 50 million in 1848, 129 million in 1873, and over 219 million by the end of the century. None of this coal was burned efficiently, and the output of smoke and soot was enormous. A thick pall hung over every one of the industrial towns, especially when the weather was bad, and the sulphurous smoke corroded the lungs and blackened the skin. Pea-soup fogs were almost permanent features of the winter scene, and unfortunately Dickens's 'London particular' could be matched in every large town.

Where heavy industry existed, conditions were far worse. The iron and steel trade vomited out great clouds of brown smoke loaded with iron oxide, whenever tempering operations were going on, and in factories producing alkalis such as soda, great clouds of hydrochloric acid gas were allowed out into the air: as the vapour is heavy it tended to drift into the streets in a corrosive fog that made the eyes sting, attacked the throat, and caused agonizing paroxysms of coughing to lungs already rendered bronchial by the general town atmosphere. Soap factories and tanneries added to the unwholesome reek of the towns: many tanneries still used enormous baths of decomposing dog dung to soften the hides before tanning.

Inside the factories, conditions were even more deadly. No precautions were taken to guard against poisonous or irritating fumes, and workers in the dusty trades universally suffered from respiratory troubles. Perhaps the worst trade of all was the cutlery grinding in Sheffield: the combination of grindstone dust and metal particles tore into the lungs like a corrosive poison. Dr. Knight, a Sheffield physician who tried nobly to stem the increasing rate of 'grinders' asthma', gave this description of it:

> They usually begin their work with the fourteenth year, and, if they have good constitutions, rarely notice any symptoms before the twentieth year. Then the symptoms of their peculiar disease appear. They suffer from shortness of breath at the slightest effort in going up hill or up stairs, they habitually raise the shoulders to relieve the permanent and increasing want of breath; they bend forward, and seem, in general, to feel most comfortable in the crouching position in which they work. Their complexion becomes dirty yellow, their features express anxiety, they complain of pressure on the chest. Their voices become rough and hoarse, they cough loudly, and the sound is as if air was driven through a wooden tube. From time to time they expectorate considerable quantities of dust, either mixed with phlegm or in balls or cylindrical masses, with a thin coating of mucus. Spitting blood, inability to lie down, night sweat, colliquative diarrhoea, unusual loss of flesh, and all the usual symptoms of consumption of the lungs finally carry them off...

Fork grinders, who ground dry and therefore breathed in more dust, both from the forks and from the grindstones, could expect to live between twenty-eight and thirty-two years at most; razor grinders, working with wet and dry wheels, could last until their forty-fifth year. There was a grim Sheffield joke that heavy drinking would prolong a grinder's life well above the average—because it kept him away from work. However, when some of the manufacturers, on the advice of Dr. Knight, and genuinely anxious to prevent this appalling mortality, put up covers over the grindstones and a simple extraction system, the workers broke them down again. Apparently they believed that if the job were made too 'soft', there would be competition for the work and wages would fall.

The general atmosphere of factories can be gathered from a comment in Mayhew's *London Labour and the London Poor*: he interviewed a sewerman who said, 'I didn't like the confinement or the close air in the factories,' so took up cesspool clearing as a welcome relief.

It is easy to sneer at one side or the other—to see the manufacturers and landlords as wicked melodramatic villains complete with top hat and riding crop, or the workers as rather vicious sheep, too ignorant to see where their own advantage lay—but it is all too easy. Society was studded with men of goodwill at all levels, from the intelligent men in 'fustian jackets' whom Engels met in working men's institutes, all the way up to the head of government, in the person of that devious, hard-working, kind-hearted genius, Benjamin Disraeli. But goodwill could not cut through the tangles of private property, parochialism, departmental jealousies, and inertia that made up the British system of government and law. Before even a survey could be made of London's decaying sewers, let alone any actual improvement, eight separate departments had to be consulted and mollified, and finally concentrated into one Board of Commissioners. While poor people in the crowded courts were suffering all the stink and disease arising from the piles of dung in the middle of the yards, there was a serious legal battle going on to decide whether it was stealing to take away the heaps. One party claimed that the heaps belonged to the landlord of the property, another that the people who had created the filth had the ownership rights in it. In either case it would obviously have been against all equity for the state to take away such a valuable possession, which could be sold to a farmer for profit. In the factories, measures for safety or comfort met with similar difficulties, because there was a general reluctance to make national legislation. The local doctors might suggest an improvement, and a good-hearted manufacturer might be prepared to institute it, but if it cost money, and were only applied locally, competitors in other towns would take advantage of the situation to undercut. Thus, spending money on welfare might in the end only produce more unemployed. This argument was of course used by unscrupulous employers to sweat their workers, but unfortunately in a *laissez-faire* society it was basically true.

From the workers' point of view, there was no question of 'withdrawing their labour' until better conditions were granted. There were always too many other people only too anxious to take over the work, however hard and unpleasant, and to live in even worse conditions. The Irish, in particular, were so used to famine and dirt at home that they found even the worst conditions in England an improvement.

'From recent enquiries on the subject, it would appear, that upwards of 20,000 individuals live in cellars in Manchester alone,' wrote Peter Gaskell, in *The Manufacturing Population of England* (1833). 'These are generally Irish families—handloom weavers, bricklayer's labourers, etc. etc., whose children are beggars or matchsellers in conjunction with their mothers. The crowds of beings that emerge from these dwellings every morning are truly astonishing, and present very little variety as to respectability of appearance; all are ragged, all are filthy, all are squalid. . . . The domestic habits of these improvident creatures are vile in the extreme. . . . The Irish cotter has brought with him his disgusting domestic companion the pig; for whenever he can scrape together a sufficient sum for the purchase of one of these animals, it becomes an inmate of his cellar. . . .'

'The Irish population of Liverpool, by the census consisting of nearly 60,000, and those of the lower class, are so notoriously dirty in their habits, that the better class of English workman will not reside in the same courts,' an enquiry was told in 1845.

Perhaps the best evidence on the habits of the Irish comes from Engels. Engels was a German visitor, with no preconceived views about the superiority of the English, Irish, or any other of the island races. His natural tendency was to blame environment for any faults in the population, as appears in his later work, written in collaboration with Marx, so he was likely to give any particularly squalid group of the population the benefit of the doubt. But when he came to the Irish . . .

The worst quarters of all the large towns are inhabited by Irishmen. Whenever a district is distinguished for especial filth and especial ruinousness, the explorer may safely count upon meeting chiefly those Celtic faces which one recognizes at the first glance as different from the Saxon physiognomy of the native, and the singing, aspirate brogue which the true Irishman never loses. I have occasionally heard the Irish-Celtic language spoken in the most thickly populated parts of Manchester. . . . Filth and drunkenness, too, they have brought with them. The lack of cleanliness, which is not so injurious in the country, where population is scattered, and which is the Irishman's second nature, becomes terrifying and gravely dangerous through its concentration here in the great cities. The Milesian [Irish labourer] deposits all garbage and filth before his house door here, as he was accustomed to do at home, and so accumulates the pools and dirt-heaps which disfigure the working-people's quarters and poison the air. He builds a pig-sty against the house wall as he did at home, and if he is prevented from doing this, he lets the pig sleep in the room with himself. . . . The filth and comfortlessness that prevail in the houses themselves it is impossible to describe. The Irishman is unaccustomed to the presence of furniture; a heap of straw, a few rags, utterly beyond use as clothing, suffice for his nightly couch. . . .

The Irish were notorious for the decrepit state of their houses, and it was not uncommon for whole streets of houses in the Irish colonies to fall down into the street, inhabitants and all. This must have been due in part to the jerry-building methods, but badly built houses were occupied by the English, too. What decayed the homes of the Irish workers was a combination of rats, encouraged by the dirt, potatoes, and rags—rats gnawed into roof and floor timbers to make hiding-places, and weakened the already shoddy house-structures—and the Irish habit of shooting all kinds of rubbish, including sewage, under the floors, where they encouraged wet rot in the woodwork. To be fair, this habit was observed with other workers; R. Scott Alison, in 1842, said of the homes of Scottish colliers:

'In some of these houses the females are so lazy and so filthy in their habits that they carry their ashes and cinders no farther than to a corner of the apartment, where they accumulate and have their bulk swollen by the addition of various impurities.'

But in general it was always the Irish who took the position at the bottom of the social heap, and their revolting standards of living were a constant threat to the native English workman who might be tempted to struggle against the employers. With such a competition going on, it is not surprising that reform of the housing and sanitary conditions took such a time, even with the threat of cholera hanging over the population.

One of the men who achieved at least a loosening of the Gordian knot which Victorian society had tied for itself was Edwin Chadwick, barrister, journalist, expert administrator and fierce opponent of bureaucracy, who lent his formidable talents to the cause of public health. Chadwick was a man with a strong and sincere vocation to help humanity, and also a passion for financial tidiness. He could write with unusual sympathy about the difficulties of the poor (as in his description of the factors which made cleanliness difficult), but he also saw a tremendous loss to the community in the numbers of widows and orphans thrown upon parish relief and the Poor Rate by the deaths of their breadwinners, usually before due time. Chadwick was a difficult man to work with, found it hard to delegate, quarrelled with all his collaborators at one time or another, and certainly made many enemies among the lethargic and smug civil service, but he succeeded by sheer effort, intelligence, and the ability to work, if necessary, eighteen hours a day. His great work, *The Report on the Sanitary Condition of the Labouring Population*, published in 1842, was the result of questionnaires to medical officers in Poor Law unions, letters to builders, police officers, surveyors, prison governors, and the preparation of maps, statistics, and comparison (for example, Chadwick found that in Derby, the expectation of life was forty-nine years for a member of the gentry, thirty-eight for a tradesman, but only twenty for a workman—this displays not only the conditions of adult life, of course, but the appalling rate of infantile mortality). The whole report was prepared in a blaze of effort. The survey showed existing conditions to be so appalling, and the recommendations for reform so uncompromising, that Chadwick's fellow-workers would not have their names on the title-page: Chadwick's appeared alone. The report became known as 'Mr. Chadwick's Report' or 'The Sanitary Report', and 10,000 copies of it were sold, an unheard-of number for a government publication at the time. It showed maps of cholera cases following the lines of the worst-drained streets, it had proposals for sewers and street-sweeping at the public cost, and it was filled with statistics, tables, and telling human stories of the effects of dirt and bad housing.

Chadwick's report set the scene for further surveys: a Royal Commission was set up to study the health of towns, and, unusually for a Royal Commission, produced two extensive reports in two years, covering conditions in fifty towns, of which only one had a satisfactory sewage system and only six a good water supply.

In spite of the surveys, in spite of the Public Health Act of 1848 and the Board of Health, government support for the idea of public health was lukewarm. It took many years, changes of government, and the goodwill of Disraeli, before the poor, in most towns and cities, finally got their drainage and water supply: Chadwick's report came out in 1842, Disraeli's Public Health Act only in 1875. There were some towns with a greater civic pride and ability to see the advantages of a healthy environment: Joseph Chamberlain, mayor of Birmingham from 1873 to 1875, worked with the slogan 'High rates and a healthy city' and forestalled the Public Health Act by starting slum clearance and the laying of proper drainage.

Even so, conditions in the towns did not improve fast. In 1883 Francis Galton, the eugenist and founder of the science of demography, could write as a well-known fact, 'It cannot be doubted that town life is harmful to the town population', and his figures show a melancholy system by which the more enterprising and intelligent countrymen are attracted to the towns by higher wages, and are then killed off by the unfavourable conditions, thus causing a constant draining away of the most capable members of the community. It was still possible to say, as Shelley remarks in *Peter Bell the Third*: 'Hell is a city much like London—a populous and smoky city.'

12. Fouling our own Nest

If the worst kind of dirt is the evidence of other people in the world, there has never been more of it than now. There are about 3,500 million other people. Every year they excrete about 59,000 million gallons of human waste on to the land and into the water.

Such figures, although interesting, do not give very much idea of the problems facing the world in disposing of the waste created by its enormous population. It is easier to grasp the human consequences if we look at the problems of water supply and disposal. All the water we have is, ultimately, stored in the oceans. It is evaporated by the sun, carried over the land areas as clouds, and comes down as rain, which runs off rock and through soil to the rivers, and thence back to the oceans again. Apart from the small amount of water extracted from the sea by desalination, we depend entirely on the rainfall for our water, for drinking, washing, industrial processes, and diluting the waste products that we produce.

On the average, in England alone, the usable rainfall that can be trapped for water supply will provide about 600 gallons per day for every man, woman, and child, but in some of the drier months this will fall to 200-300 gallons. Where piped water is available, which is, in England, a very large proportion of the country, people tend to use about 50 gallons per day per person. In other words, during the drier months, we may use up to a quarter of the total water available to us, contaminate it, and then have to clean it up before we can return it to the rivers. This is an average figure for the whole of England, and therefore includes sparsely populated rural areas where there is ample water: in the teeming south-east, in a dry month, we may be contaminating up to half of all our available water with dirt, sewage, detergents, industrial waste, and so on.

This means in practice that we have to use the water two or three times before it completes its journey from the hills to the sea. Along the Thame and the Thames, for example, there are three major areas where water is taken in for use, contaminated, passed to sewage works for purification, and then passed out into the river for use by the next centre of population. Sometimes only a few miles of river separates the outfall from one sewage works and the inflow pipe for the next water authority. In west London, where much of the water is taken in from the Thames at Laleham, near Staines, a considerable proportion of the water has already been used by people in Oxford and Reading, Luton, and other big centres of population. If the sewage works and water purification units stopped working for even a day or so, Londoners would be drinking the bath water, and worse, of their north-westerly neighbours, and not diluted by a very large amount of river water, either.

It is no coincidence that the growth of cities and the multiplication of other people has led to a corresponding increase in the sales of soaps, detergents, cosmetics and toilet preparations, and all the other materials that serve to make human life a little less nasty and brutish. The Industrial Revolution, which made the towns grimy and the air polluted, also provided, as a small recompense, cheap sodium carbonate and therefore the means for making good quality soap. While other manufacturers concentrated on producing the soap as well and inexpensively as possible, William Hesketh Lever appealed directly to the consumer, selling the vision of a better life to those Victorian housewives struggling desperately against the smoke, the smells, the general squalid hopelessness of the towns. That his soap was no better than that of Joseph Crosfield or William Gossage was irrelevant: Lever had found the magic key to the housewives' hearts, and purses, and eventually swallowed up most of the other soapmakers into his empire, first Lever Brothers and then Unilever. The techniques for selling dreams to housewives have become increasingly sophisticated and subtle: much of the soap has remained exactly the same.

Modern advertising and marketing methods have always been closely associated with the soap and detergents industry, partly because the products themselves are very suitable for mass-marketing methods. They are stable for long periods in shops, unlike most foods, they are bought by almost every household, regularly, and used up, so that there is a constant turnover of the stock, and they are susceptible to minor and unimportant changes in pack, colour, perfume, and ingredients, which do little or nothing practical for the customer, but help to keep up the excitement and make an excuse for more advertising. Soaps and detergents also respond well to modern advertising methods because they appeal to the deep-rooted fear of defilement in all of us: they promise that life (with the new product, of course) will be a little cleaner, a little safer, a little less ignobly animal in its details. A new food product, on the other hand, can only appeal easily to our present appetites, not our dreams. (I realize that this is not entirely true: some foods are presented as adjuncts to the Good Life, so that we can feel that in buying and eating them we are sharing an experience with the rich and successful. However, they do not offer the same opportunities for 'depth' advertising as cleansing products.) A great deal of detergent and toiletry advertising is directed to fears—fear of rejection ('His best friends won't tell him', 'Colgate gives the Ring of Confidence'), or of disease, or of being thought inferior. Much of the advertising for washing powders is designed to make housewives feel that they are neglectful wives and mothers unless they wash their family's clothes with the particular powder offered. It is perhaps rather difficult to appeal directly to the fear of contamination by other people, because the advertisements would have to be rather too explicit about the type of contamination. (And, of course, some readers or viewers of the advertisements might identify themselves with the 'other people' and be offended.) It can be done, however. Most of the advertisements that harp on the fear of 'germs' tend to imply obliquely that the germs originate from other people.

The fact that soaps and detergents appeal to a very deep human need, the need for decontamination, has made them big business and big advertising appropriations. There is a healthy sign, however, that the public are beginning to tire of having their psyches manipulated by the detergent companies and advertising agencies: in a survey conducted by the manipulators' own body, the Institute of Practitioners in Advertising, it was reported that, of types of commercial *particularly disliked*, cleaning and washing products had a clear lead.*

Unfortunately, in all this activity, not much thought was given to the effects of the cleaning products when they went down the sink and into the sewerage system. The banks of foam on our rivers, prior to 1964, became higher and higher as the use of synthetic detergents increased. Soap is broken down easily by bacteria, and therefore ceases to foam or behave at all like a washing agent, almost before it leaves the house drainage system. Synthetic detergents, on the other hand, are more or less resistant to bacteria, and thus pass through, not only the drains, but the bacterial digestion processes in the sewage works. In the so-called 'activated sludge' plants, where air is pumped through the sewage to speed up oxidation of waste materials, the effects of too much detergent were shown by enormous clouds of foam as the air passed through—not the white shimmering foam of the television commercials, but a dirty brown foam that contained most of the other ingredients of the sewage. Sometimes, in a high wind, these filthy clouds would take off and float gently over the countryside, eventually landing like an enormous cow-pat in someone's garden. Weirs, and other points on the rivers where the water was churned up, became covered with foam, and at Castleford, in Yorkshire, clouds of foam often filled the streets as the wind blew it away from the river.

In the USA similar troubles occurred, but there conditions were even worse, because many of the rural areas have very inadequate sewage arrangements. Housewives found foaming water coming from their taps: this was because detergents from the septic tanks and drains had found their way into springs and artesian wells supplying the drinking water. The presence of the foam was an uneasy reminder that all the other contents of the drains and sewers must also have seeped into the water supply, but local authorities found it more convenient to attack the

* 'As Others See Us', IPA Occasional Paper 17.

detergent manufacturers. There was even talk, incredible for the Land of the Free, of banning synthetic detergents altogether. Fortunately for them, the detergent manufacturers found different types of material that were more easily broken down by bacteria (though not entirely, even now) and gave us the magic words 'biodegradable' or 'biologically soft' to describe these new detergents. In the United Kingdom, the Ministry of Housing and Public Works came to an agreement with the detergent manufacturers that these improved materials would be used from 1964 onwards. Rivers do not foam as much as they used to, but they are by no means free of the nuisance, as a quick look at the river Wandle, which comes into the Thames at Battersea, will show. Activated sludge plants still foam, but less. Unfortunately, even small traces of detergent tend to stop the rivers taking up oxygen efficiently, and oxygen is essential if the water is to purify itself. As in many other periods in history, we have added to the convenience of our homes with these new products, only at the expense of our water supplies.

Water pollution caused by industrial processes can be even more devastating than that caused by household wastes, because the variety of the materials is so much wider, and some of them may be really deadly poisons, such as one would not use in the home anyway. This problem is not new, of course. In Spenser's *Faerie Queene* he describes the river Dart as 'nigh choked with sands of tinny mines' or the washings from tin extraction. As these muds usually contain lead and zinc salts, which are very poisonous to all forms of life, this particular pollution must have killed off all the fish and anyone foolish enough to drink much of the water. Gasworks waste, fed into the rivers during the nineteenth century, finally killed off those famous salmon that had been fattening on human waste for so many centuries. They have not yet returned to the Thames and the Mersey, but the Severn, running through less industrialized country, is now fairly well stocked. As for the Tyne and Tees, which run through the heart of the heavy chemical industry, it must be a matter of definition whether the liquid that passes under the bridges is properly called water at all. The Irwell is much as Engels found it in 1844. Jeremy Bugler, of the *Observer*, reported in February 1970:

'The Irwell is one of the most blighted stretches of moving

water in Britain; for long it has carried out a contest with Birmingham's River Tame for the title of the United Kingdom's most ruined river. No fish can swim in it, nor livestock drink its water. And if you fall into the Irwell, you will be rushed to hospital and stomach-pumped. While I was looking last week at the foetid swill of the Manchester Ship Canal (which at that part was the Irwell canalized), a police patrolman was moved enough to get out of his car and tell me: "Don't fall in there, you'll ruin my afternoon."'

Many of our waterways could make a serious challenge to the Irwell to be Miss Pollution of the 1970s. Pollution with industrial waste is, of course, illegal, but it is difficult to prove that the chemicals found lower down the river actually originated from any particular plant. I have heard the management of a large factory, in an international group with a high reputation for public service, congratulating themselves that a ton or so of waste dyestuffs had 'gone into the canal' without observation, so the practices in other factories may be imagined. Even when pollution is proved, the fines imposed are tiny compared with the cost of installing proper waste-disposal plant: early in 1970, the enormous Fison's chemical complex was fined the crippling sum of £50 and £10 costs for polluting the river Gipping with DDT, a poison capable of killing all the fish and most other living creatures in the river, and possibly affecting its ecology for years.

Paper and paper-making are particularly deadly to rivers: the wood-pulp which forms the basis for paper uses up a lot of oxygen, and therefore makes for shortages in oxygen for purifying other materials in the water, while the sulphite liquor that is used to extract cellulose from the wood-pulp actually combines with oxygen and can make river water totally incapable of purifying itself. In the United Kingdom this is not such a serious hazard, but in the USA there is virtually no control over the wood-pulp users, and this is one of the reasons why Lake Erie (to name only one example) has become a stinking, airless swamp, incapable of supporting the life of fish or any other creatures except rather disgusting algae. Industrial pollution has become so widespread, and so varied, as technological changes occur, that at least one authority on water treatment, Professor H. B. N. Hynes, has suggested that we may have to allow the use of some rivers in our industrial areas *entirely* for the disposal of industrial waste, so as to save the others for the community.* In other words, some of our rivers must become open drains again.

One of the most worrying features about such waste disposal is that tipping some poisonous or other material into the river is not the end of the affair. Some materials, quite harmless in themselves, can affect river life adversely: phosphates, from fertilizers and detergents, are harmless to life, and even beneficial, but unfortunately they encourage such an overwhelming growth of algae and slime moulds that the river water becomes saturated with these lower forms of life which cut off the oxygen from fish. Other harmful effects can arise from chemical reactions between two or more different pollutants, or between pollutants and water-treatment chemicals. Rotterdam drinking water tastes so peculiarly bad because it comes from the Rhine, and the German chemical industry fouls the Rhine with phenols from coal-tar and similar sources. These would not taste so badly by themselves, but the water is also fouled with untreated sewage, and has to be chlorinated. This converts the phenols into chlorinated phenols, which have a penetrating taste and smell, like disinfectant, detectable at very low concentrations. The situation in this case is unpleasant, but not dangerous, but there are so many possibilities of interaction between the various materials that are discharged into our rivers that it is surprising that we have not had more serious trouble. To take one example that is theoretically possible: organic phosphates are used very widely in modern insecticides and similar treatments for plants: Malathion, Parathion, Azinphos-methyl, Carbophenothion, Chlorthion, Demeton-S-methyl, Dichlorvos, Dimethoate, Disulphoton, Ethion, Fenchlorphos, Fenitrothion, Mevinphos, Phenkapton, Phosphamidon and Thiometon are only some of the insecticides in this group of chemicals, and they are ingredients in many mixtures sold to farmers and gardeners.

Fluorine compounds are discharged from aluminium works and similar plants, and organic fluorides are used in lubricants and metal finishes (such as non-stick finishes for frying-pans and so on). The compounds of fluorine and organic phosphates are not used in this way, because they are deadly poisons: they are,

* *The Biology of Polluted Waters*, Liverpool University Press, 1963.

in fact, related to the 'nerve gases' that can immobilize the nervous system (and hence, rapidly, the heart, brain, and the rest of living matter) in tiny doses. They are so deadly in fact that, like the nuclear bomb, they are too dreadful to handle. What, now, if organo-fluoride residues, 'lost into the canal', meet residues of an organic phosphate from an insecticide factory, or are washed out of the fields of some over-enthusiastic farmer into the same river? It is not the set of conditions that a chemist would *choose* to make a fluorophosphonate, the poisonous material, but it could work well enough to produce the microscopic doses necessary for deaths to occur. They would probably be recorded as heart failure unless the doctor knew more about the fluorophosphonates than most medical men. And this is only one of the permutations of unplanned reactions between industrial effluents.

It is ironic that every new advance in our technological standard of living seems to provide new waste products to foul our water supply. Chromium from metal-plating and tanning is a poison to all types of river life; phosphates from detergents, although not poisonous, encourage the growth of algae and slime-moulds which themselves foul the water; gasworks produce thiocyanates which are unpleasant in themselves, and are converted to the poisonous cyanogen chloride when the water is chlorinated. This material is about as poisonous as prussic acid. One of the new hazards which faces the ecologist and water-treatment engineer is the possibility of radio-active waste escaping into rivers. Radio-active materials are now used not only in power stations, hospitals, and 'defence' laboratories, but in such mundane jobs as checking the levels of liquids in bottles in a packaging line, or finding out whether a new cosmetic really does 'feed the skin'. Sooner or later, someone is going to have an accident with one of these radio-active materials, it will go down the sink or into the sewer, and we shall have to learn to live with radio-active bacteria in our water-treatment plants. It is not surprising that companies expose themselves and us to these risks and inconveniences. The profits from a successful new luxury product are enormous, the fines imposed for contamination of the rivers are petty.

The air over our cities, at least since the Clean Air Act of 1956, has become less dark and obviously dirty, and the

'London particular' has virtually disappeared—a matter of perverse disappointment to many foreign visitors brought up on Dickens and Edgar Wallace.

In some cities the effects of the Act have been better than in others: one can only assume that the Act does not apply at all in Rotherham, for example, which is shrouded in dirty brown smoke like something in a Cruickshank illustration. Some of the aerial pollution is 'clean' but none the less offensive: around Middlesbrough and its neighbouring industrial towns the clean air of the moors, at some miles from the centres of population, is subtly sharpened with ammonia gas from the enormous fertilizer plants: where this meets the sulphur dioxide fumes from other factory chimneys, a soft rain of ammonium sulphate descends on the countryside. As this material is quite a good fertilizer in itself, the grass grows remarkably well in lines and patterns, not controlled by the dancing of fairies, but by the prevailing air currents bringing the two contaminants together.

The last 'London particular' was an object lesson: it occurred in December 1952, starting as a white fog on Thursday morning, 4 December. Buses and cars crept along with pedestrians walking in front. A duck, flying blind, crashed through the glass roof of Victoria station and fell at the feet of the crowds of waiting passengers. At a greyhound stadium the dogs lost sight of the hare, only a yard or two ahead, and the race had to be abandoned (it took half an hour to find the dogs again). At Sadler's Wells *La Traviata* ended in confusion because so much fog had seeped into the auditorium that the singers could not see the conductor. A plane at London Airport made a perfect landing with instruments, and then disappeared: the pilot had got lost trying to taxi to the terminal.

By Friday the fog was brown, and on Saturday black. Old people, hopelessly lost, died of exposure. Most people, however, were suffering from the high concentration of sulphur dioxide concentrated in the fog: all our fuels—coal, oil, and so on—contain sulphur compounds, and these burn to sulphur dioxide. The fog prevented the smoke and fumes from escaping, and the sulphur dioxide attacked the lungs. By Saturday noon, in that December fog, the London hospitals were full of bronchial cases, many of whom never recovered from the effects of the fog.

Sulphur dioxide still forms a part of our industrial atmosphere, and it still has its baneful influence on our lungs. The natives say grimly that the morning chorus of Manchester and Newcastle is the sound of sparrows coughing.

The motor-car also adds its contribution to our city atmospheres, particularly of carbon monoxide and nitrous fumes. Carbon monoxide is, of course, a well-known poison, but the limits set for safety by various authorities vary enormously. In America the limits vary between 30 parts per million (in California) to 100 parts per million in many other states. In Russia the limit was set at 2 parts per million, and it has been recommended that this be dropped to 1 part per million. It would be uncharitable to suggest that these figures represent a fair measure of the power of the car industry in the two countries, but most unbiased authorities on air pollution would favour the Russian figure.

Nitrous fumes also cause lung damage, but may also cause deeper ills: they appear to attack the nervous system as well. Not enough work has been done on this aspect to set limits for nitrous fumes, but while the doctors and biochemists are arguing and the car industry is stalling, cars are belching out nitrous fumes. No doubt we shall know soon what they have been doing to us.

Meanwhile, the atmosphere in our cities, despite the Clean Air Act, remains so characteristically dirty that, it is said, doctors carrying out post mortems on unknown bodies usually assume that anyone with pink lungs is a recent immigrant. The native British have black lungs.

Modern life presents other complications to the doctors when the occasional epidemics strike. Although standards of public health have risen enormously in the last century, we have introduced new hazards. There are not only many more people, but they mix more. In the days of plague or cholera, the disease would strike a small community and make its way around the families: travellers could carry it farther afield, but there were not many travellers and they moved slowly, so diseases spread in an almost dilatory way. Now a businessman can fly back from a conference in, say, Nigeria, spend the evening with his family, take a train to London with a crowd of other travellers the next morning, squeeze into the tube train with fifty others, talk to his office colleagues, have lunch with another group, travel home with a hundred other strangers, and perhaps go out to dinner or a theatre with yet more people. In twenty-four hours he can be in close contact with perhaps 200 to 300 people, all of whom will then return home to their communities, contacting more strangers on the way. If our businessman had brought back with him the germ of, say, pneumonic plague, a thousand others, in perhaps fifty different districts, could be infected in a day, before the original carrier even felt ill. This is the nightmare of the immigration officer and the Medical Officer of Health.

The same dangers apply to food poisoning, which is usually a direct result of dirt in the handling of food. No longer can the Medical Officer draw a circle round the known cases of food poisoning and expect to find the offending bakery or pie shop in the middle.

In the face of all these dangers, one would expect public buildings, restaurants, and all the other places where people congregate to be especially clean. It seems to make as much sense as looking both ways before crossing a London street. Unfortunately, as a recent survey by Messrs Reckitt and Colman has shown, cleanliness is not the outstanding impression that visitors gain from Britain.

'Some of the buildings were clean but others looked grubby. Even Buckingham Palace could use a clean up. I think it detracts from the tourist value. It really looks crummy . . .'

Sometimes the first public building that a visitor sees is a railway station: one hopes that they are not all like this:

'We had something to eat in the café there and it all seemed unclean which made me feel disagreeable and I wouldn't eat there again . . . the walls seemed dirty, the tables were wet. The floor seemed to have many things on it and the staff seemed unclean.'

Such comments are not only made by hypercritical visitors, as is shown by a similar report, made by the same company, on attitudes of the British public to the cleanliness of public buildings:

'The tubes are cleaner than British Railways. You may go on the Bakerloo Line and say that it was dirty, but if you go on the

Broad Street train, it's filthy, the windows are dirty, you can't see out of them.'

'You get your hands black with actual dirt.'

'They're certainly not places that you'd want to sit in [railway waiting rooms]. I'd rather stand on a platform than wait in there and sit down. It seems to be years before they paint a station.'*

This shabbiness and grubbiness of much of our public transport, public buildings, streets, offices, and many restaurants, is the besetting disease of the twentieth century in 'advanced' countries. It is obviously not as bad as the filth and danger of earlier times, but it arises from the same source: too much concentration on individual comfort and profit, too much parochial thinking, too much departmental or business rivalry, and not enough thought about the needs of the community. The sad thing is that modern communications—television, glossy magazines, easy travel—have made us all more aware of the grace and elegance which can be imparted to life by modern technology, and the advertisers do their best to see that we spend most of our private resources on bringing some of these improvements into our own homes. This makes the contrast even more acute between the ideal of the advertisers' dream home and the reality of the shabby street in which it stands. And because it is easier and more profitable to sell gadgets and frills than to make real improvements to the quality of life, we have the situation of an enormous industry spending millions of pounds per year to try to persuade us to buy new cars or even new gadgets for cars, while our trains are filthy and out-of-date, and our buses are equally unwelcoming. Similarly, our soap companies sell us, for the home, a bewildering range of products —each one advertised, at great expense to the community, so as to 'create a demand'—while in most of our public lavatories the basic 'demand' for soap, any soap, and hot water and a clean towel, is not met. We create a huge industry putting food in cans for dogs, and then allow people to 'take them for walks' so that they can defecate on the public streets. We spend, as a community, nearly thirty pounds per year for each man, woman,

---

* Quotations from *The Pilot Attitude Survey on Public Attitudes to Cleanliness in Public Buildings and Areas* and *How Clean do Others See Us?*, Interflow Ltd.

and child, on packaging materials, and occupy some of our most lively minded citizens to design and manufacture the packages—then we find them littered over our beaches and countryside, and use nineteenth-century methods to remove them from our homes.

Our attitudes, in fact, are no different from those of the eighteenth-century gentry who fitted water-closets in their houses, but did not bother where the contents went after they had pulled the chain. Cars, cleaning products, pet foods and glossy packages are not bad things in themselves, any more than the water-closets were bad things, but our priorities are misplaced: we are making our homes elegant and convenient while making our whole environment more shabby, dirty, and ultimately hostile to human life. A love of ostentation and luxury is natural to human beings, and is a very likeable human weakness. Perhaps we can direct this basic impulse to the creation of cleaner and more beautiful cities, an unlittered countryside, water fit to drink and air fit to breathe.

Select Bibliography

It would be manifestly impossible to list all the sources and allied material consulted or used in the writing of this book, but the following list may be of value to the reader who wishes to go further in the history of everyday life at various periods. Books marked * are particularly recommended for their detailed references to primary sources.

PRE-NORMAN

Bede (trans. Leo Sherley-Price), *A History of the English Church and People.* Penguin Books, 1955

MEDIEVAL

M. R. James, *Abbeys.* Great Western Railway, 1925
Johannes Nohl (trans. C. H. Clarke), *The Black Death.* Unwin, 1961
The Paston Letters (ed. John Warrington). Everyman's Library, Dent, 1956
F. Rörig (trans. Don Bryant), *The Mediaeval Town.* Batsford, 1967
*Philip Ziegler, *The Black Death.* Collins, 1969

ELIZABETHAN

John Buxton, *Elizabethan Taste.* Macmillan, 1963
*M. St. Clare Byrne, *Elizabethan Life in Town and Country.* Methuen, 8th ed. 1961
Thomas Deloney, *Jack of Newberie.* In *Shorter Elizabethan Novels* ed. George Saintsbury. Everyman's Library, Dent, 1966

John Stow (ed. H. B. Wheatley), *The Survey of London*. Every-man's Library, Dent 1956

Lytton Strachey, *Elizabeth and Essex*. Chatto & Windus, 1928

JACOBEAN, COMMONWEALTH, RESTORATION

The Memoirs of Ann, Lady Fanshawe. John Lane the Bodley Head, 1907

*Robert Ashton, *James I by His Contemporaries*. Hutchinson, 1969

Elizabeth Burton, *The Jacobeans at Home*. Secker & Warburg, 1962

Daniel Defoe (ed. Anthony Burgess & Christopher Bristow), *A Journal of the Plague Year*. Penguin Books, 1966

Philip Erlanger (trans. Lionel Smith-Gordon), *George Villiers, Duke of Buckingham*. Hodder & Stoughton, 1953

John Evelyn (ed. William Bray), *Diary*. Everyman's Library, Dent, 1966

William McElwee, *The Wisest Fool in Christendom*. Faber & Faber, 1958

Samuel Pepys (ed. H. B. Wheatley), *Diary*. G. Bell, 1952

GEORGIAN

Boswell's London Journal (ed. F. A. Pottle). Heinemann, 1950

J. L. and Barbara Hammond, *The Skilled Labourer*. Longmans Green, 1925

—— *The Town Labourer*. Longmans Green, 1925

—— *The Village Labourer*. Longmans Green, 1927

*M. Dorothy George, *London Life in the Eighteenth Century*. Kegan Paul, Trench & Trubner, 1925

W. Eden Hooper, *The History of Newgate and the Old Bailey*. Underwood Press, 1935

Hugh Phillips, *Mid-Georgian London*. Collins, 1964

—— *The Thames about 1750*. Collins, 1951

VICTORIAN

*Frederick Engels (trans. Institute of Marxism-Leninism, Moscow), *The Condition of the Working Class in England in 1844*. rev. ed. Panther, 1969

Norman Longmate, *King Cholera*. Hamish Hamilton, 1966

Henry Mayhew, *London Labour and the London Poor*. Frank Cass, 1967

Henry Mayhew, (ed. Peter Quennell), *Mayhew's Characters.* Paul Hamlyn, 1951
——— ——— *Mayhew's London.* Paul Hamlyn, 1956
——— ——— *London's Underworld.* Paul Hamlyn, 1967
*E. Royston Pike, *Human Documents of the Industrial Revolution in Britain.* George Allen & Unwin, 1966
*——— *Human Documents of the Victorian Golden Age,* George Allen & Unwin, 1967

SPECIALIZED
N. J. Barton, *The Lost Rivers of London.* Leicester University Press, 1962
Brendan Lehane, *The Compleat Flea.* John Murray, 1969
John Pudney, *The Smallest Room.* Michael Joseph, 1959
J. F. D. Shrewsbury, *The Plague of the Philistines.* Gollancz, 1964
E. S. Turner, *Taking the Cure.* Michael Joseph, 1967
Lawrence Wright, *Clean and Decent.* Routledge & Kegan Paul, 1960

Index

Index

Agnes, St., 11
Agricultural revolution, the, 120–2
Aire, river, 139
Alison, R. Scott, 154
Alum, 77, 78
Ambergris, 44, 45
Anchorites (anachorets), 11, 14
Anne, Queen, 42, 103
Anstey, Christopher, 108
Antony of Thebais, 11
Aqueducts, 7–8
Arkwright, Sir Richard, 119
Artisan, The, 132–3
Asthma, grinders', 150–1
Asceticism, 11
Athanasius, 11
Atmospheric pollution, 149–50, 163–5
Aubrey, John, 78, 89 n., 109

Bacon, Sir Francis, 48
Baker, Sir Richard, 64 n.: on the Black Death, 15, 23
Balzac, 128
Banner's Patent Drain Trap, 109–10
Barclay, Alexander, on table manners at court, 41
Barry, Dr. David, 145
Bath (*Aquae Sulis*), 9, 10, 107–8, 111: taking the waters, 108
Baths, 106–7: Roman, 7–10, 34; Turkish, 8, 34–6; stews, 36–8; decline of baths, 38–40; public baths, 138
Beardsley, Aubrey, 5

Bed-bugs, *see* Bugs
Bede, Venerable, 17
Benedict, St., 11, 14
Bentley, Nathaniel, and the Dirty Warehouse, 122–6
Bentley, Thomas, 122, 124
Berkeley Castle, 32
Bermondsey, 134: cholera in, 140
Bishop, John, petitions against obstructions in Thames, 65–6
Black Death, the, 15–18, 81, 82, 147: beginnings in; Central Asia, 17; in England, 15, 17–18, 23–6; economic consequences, 25–6; 'The Dance of Death', 26–7
Blake, William, 102, 126
Blencowe, Mrs. Anne, 77–8
Boccaccio, 20, 31: on the plague, 16, 26
Boke of Curtasye, on table manners, 41
Book of the Thousand Nights and One Night, 35 and n.
Boswell, James, 111 and n.
Bottesford, and the plague, 81
Boydell, John, 104
Bradford: growth of population, 131; water-carriers, 137; water supply, 139–40
Bramah water-closets, 110, 139
Brantôme, Seigneur de, 53
Brighton ('Brighthelmstone'), sea-bathing, 107
Bristol, 54, 95: and the Black Death, 18, 23; soap, 43; foul streets, 101
British Mediaeval Population (Russell), 23

Browne, Dr. Joseph, 107
Bubonic plague, 16–27, 81–8, 104: early waves, 17; Black Death, 15–18; 23–7, 81, 82; *gavoccioli* (tumours), 16–17; 'tokens', 17; epidemics since Black Death, 18, 81–3: Great Plague (1665), 18, 83–8, 90, 91, 95; nineteenth and early twentieth century, 18; plague germ, 19; fleas, 19–20, 81, 88; rats, 19, 88, 94, 95; contemporary explanations, 20–1; charms and magic against it, 21; scapegoats, 21; the flagellants, 22, 27; 'cures' and prophylactics, 22–3, 25
Buck, S. and N., panoramas of London (1749), 96–7
Bugler, Jeremy, 160–1
Bugs, 126–9: bug-catchers, 127–8
Burleigh, Lord, 65
Burney, Fanny, 107

Caius, John, on sweating sickness, 56–8
Campion, Thomas, 60
Caracalla, baths of, 7
Carbon monoxide, 165
Carew, Sir Francis, 109
Carlisle, Earl of, 74
Carlisle, water-carriers, 137
Carlyle, Thomas, 69
Carr, Robert, Earl of Somerset, 67, 71, 74
Cartwright, Edmund, 119
Castleford, and foam pollution, 159
Castor (perfume), 44, 45
Catherine of Siena, St., 23
Chadwick, (Sir) Edwin: on lack of water for working families, 135–6; Sanitary Report, 154–5
Chaloner, Thomas, and alum in Yorkshire, 78
Chamberlain, Joseph, 155
Charles I, 78, 79, 82, 83
Charles II, 89, 90, 96, 103, 104
Charlotte, Princess, and bed-bugs, 127, 128
Chatsworth, 'batheing room', 106–7
Chaucer, Geoffrey, 31, 40
Chesterfield, Lord, 111, 114
Cholera (*cholera vibrio*), 104, 140–8: spreads from India, 140; characteristics, 140–1; carried in contaminated water, 141, 147–8; breaks out in Sunderland (1831), 142–6; spreads

through country, 146; supposed remedies, 146–7; later epidemics, 147, 148
Chorlton-on-Medlock water carriers, 137
Christian IV, King of Denmark, 72–3
Chwolson, 17
Cimex lectularius (bed-bug), 126
Civet, 44–6: trade in, 46
Clanny, Dr. Reid, 142–4
Clean Air Act (1956), 163–5
Clean and Decent (Wright), 38
Clifford, Lady Anne, 79
Close stools, 49–50
Coal and coal-burning, 74–6, 103: mining, 75; conditions in pits, 136–7; cholera in mining districts, 146; and atmospheric pollution, 149; Scottish colliers' homes, 154
Coal Mines Regulation Act (1842), 136
Cobbett, William, 121: on farms and farmhouses, 120, 121
Cockroaches, 114
Coleridge, Samuel Taylor, 121
'Collective Unconscious', the, 21
Condition of the Working Class in England in 1844, The (Engels), 132
Cooke, Andrew, bug-destroyer, 127
Coprolegny, 5
Corbet, Richard, Bishop of Norwich, 79
Country conditions: in Middle Ages, 29–30: in eighteenth century, 101–2
Country houses in Tudor period, 47–9: dirty floors, 48–9
Crabbe, George, 102
Creighton, Dr., 11–12
Crome Yellow (Huxley), 53
Crompton, Samuel, 119
Cromwell, Oliver, 69, 104
Crosfield, Joseph, 157
Crusaders, the: and leprosy, 12–13; and Turkish baths, 34
Cummings, Alexander, and patent water-closet, 110
Cutlery grinders and respiratory troubles, 150–1

Dart, river, and early industrial pollution, 160
Davies, Sir John, 49
Davy, Sir Humphry, 42
Decameron (Boccaccio), 16, 20, 21

Defoe, Daniel, 82–4, 88 n.
De Fonteney, on James I, 70
Dekker, Thomas, 30, 45
Derby, expectation of life in, 154
De Saussure, 106
Detergents, 157–60: creation of foam, 159–60; and pollution, 159–60; biodegradable, 160
De Veil, Sir Thomas, 101
Dickens, Charles, 138, 149, 164
Dietz, Phillipus, on the flagellants, 22
Diocletian, baths of, 7
Directions to Servants (Swift), 100, 115–16
Dirty Dick's, Bishopsgate, 125
Dirty Warehouse, the, Leadenhall Street, 123–5
Disraeli, Benjamin, 151, 155
Dissertation Concerning the Use of Sea-Water in Diseases of the Glands, A (Russell), 107
Doe, Sir Charles, 87
Donne, John, 80
Dowland, John, 60
Down and Out in Paris and London (Orwell), 128
Dryden, John, 112
Dunciad (Pope), 99

Early Christians' rejection of cleanliness, 10–11
Edinburgh: disposal of filth, 100, 101, 133; conditions in nineteenth century, 132–3; Regulations under 1848 Police Act, 133; cholera, 146
Edward II, 32
Edward III, 15, 18, 28
Edward IV, 47
Edward VI, 50
Eggley, Ann, 136–7
Elizabeth I, 50, 55, 64, 65, 74, 79; and Harington's water-closet, 52, 53; monthly baths, 53
Elizabeth and Essex (Strachey), 52
Eltham Palace, stews, 36
Elwin, Rev. Whitwell, 137–8
Engels, Friedrich, 132, 134–5, 139, 151, 160: on the Irish in England, 152–3
English Humourists, The (Thackeray), 117
English Social History (Trevelyan), 101
Epigrammes (Davies), 49

Erasmus, on dirty floors in England, 48–9, 58
Ergotism, 26–7
Erie, Lake, pollution of, 161
Erskine, Sir Thomas, 79
Essay on Population (Malthus), 142
Essay on Waterworks (Lucas), 106
Etheldreda, Queen, 17
Etherege, Sir George, 90
Être et le Néant, L' (Sartre), 2
Evelyn, John, 96: on plague in 1625, 82; on the Great Plague, 84, 85; on the Fire of London, 93–4; on effects of coal fires, 103
Exeter, cholera in, 146

Factories, 120, 131: conditions in, 150–2
Fanshawe, Sir Richard, 88
Felton, John, 74
Fiennes, Celia, 106–7
Fire of London (1666), 92–4, 98: subsequent rebuilding, 94, 96–7
Fires: of coal, 74–6, 103; of wood, 74, 76
Flagellants, the, 22, 27
Fleas, 19–20, 49, 55, 80–1, 114: and plague, 19–20, 81, 88
Fleet River (Fleet Ditch), 28, 98, 99: choked by sewage, 27, 31; partially covered in (1539), 60; Ben Jonson on, 60–2; widening, 98–9; Fleet Canal, 99
Fleetwood, Sir William, 89 n., 90, 100
Fletcher, Giles, 60
Floors and dirt, 48–9
Foam caused by detergents, 159–60
Fogs, 149, 164
Food poisoning, 166
Forestus Alcmarianos, 20–1
Francis I of France, 32, 53–4
Frosts on Thames, 64

Galton (Sir), Francis, 16, 155
Galway, Ann, 134
Gammer Gurton's Needle, 29
Garderobes, 31–2
Gaskell, Peter, 152
Gateshead, cholera in, 146
Gathin, Jeuan, on the Black Death, 15, 16
Gay, John, 80
George I, 39

Gibbon, Edward, 10, 14: on Roman baths, 71; on habits of early Christians, 10–11
Gilchrist, hairdresser, 113–14
Gin-drinking, 111–12
Gipping, river, polluted by DDT, 161
Glasgow, cholera in, 146
Glasgow Medical Journal, 147
Gondomar, Count, 72
Gossage, William, 157
Granville, Dr. A. B., 146
Great Coggeshall, Essex, and the plague, 81–2
Great Plague (1665), 18, 83–8, 90, 91, 95: orders for shutting up houses, 86–8; orders for cleansing streets, 87
'Great Stink', the (1858), 148
Greenock, conditions in 1842, 134
Greville, Charles, on cholera epidemic (1831), 143–6
Gulliver's Travels (Swift), 116–17

Hadrian's Wall, Roman baths, 9
Hairdressing fashions and vermin, 113–14
Hammām, *see* Turkish baths
Hampstead Ponds, 106
Harington, Sir John, 49–53: invention of valve water-closets, 50–3, 109; recommends daily baths, 53; on entertainment at court for Christian IV, 72–3
Hawksmoor, Nicholas, 96
Health of Towns Committee, 1840, *Report*, 131 and nn.
Henry IV, 39
Henry VIII, 37, 56, 60, 64, 79: washing of his clothes, 44
Henry of Herford, on the flagellants, 22
Hidden Persuaders, The (Packard), 2
Hogarth, William, 101
Household Words, 125
Howell, James, on Paris streets, 67
Hugh of Lincoln, St., 11–12
Huis Clos (Sartre), 6
Humphrey Clinker (Smollett), 1–8
Hungary, cholera in, 142
Huxley, Aldous, 53
Hynes, Professor H. B. N., 161–2

India, cholera in, 140
Industrial pollution of waterways,

160–3: illegality, 161; small fines, 161; wood-pulp, 161; organic phosphates, 162–3; fluorine compounds, 162–3; hazards of new waste products, 163; radio-active methods, 163
Industrial Revolution, the, 119–20, 131, 136, 157
Institute of Practitioners in Advertising, 159
Irish workers in England, 152–4
Irk, river, 139
Irwell, river, pollution of, 139, 160–1

Jakes, *see* Privies
James I, 50, 67–74, 79, 83: shortcomings, 69–70; homosexuality, 70–1; weak head for liquor, 72
James II, 83
Jerome, St., 11
Jewish hygienic laws, 5–6
Jonson, Ben, 37: mock-heroic poem on Fleet Ditch, 60–2, 97
Journal of the Plague Year, A (Defoe), 82–3
Jung, and the 'Collective Unconscious', 21

Kell, Dr. James Butler, 142–4
Kelston, Harington's water-closet at, 50, 52
Kingsley, Charles, 140, 148
Knight, Dr., and grinders' asthma, 150–1
Knights of the Bath, ritual of installation, 39–40
Krafft-Ebing, 4

Lamb, A. J., 14
Lancet, 146
Lane, John, early soap-maker, 43
Laundering, 76–8
Laurie, Dr., 134
Lawrence, Sir John, 87
Laystalls, 97–8
Lazar-houses, 13–14
Leeds: growth of population, 131; pollution of water supply, 139
Leonardo da Vinci, 32–4: proposals for sewage disposal, 32; design for lavatory, 32–3; hot-water system, 34
Leprosy, 11–14: spread by the Crusades, 12–13; leper-hospitals, 13–14

Lever, William Hesketh (Visc. Lever-
hulme), 157
Leviticus, book of, 5–6, 13
Lice, 49, 54–7: types, 54–5; and typhus,
55–6; and sweating sickness, 56, 57
Lighting of streets, 102
Linen, whitening, 77–8
Liverpool: baths and wash-houses, 138;
Irish population, 152
Locks on Thames, 63, 65
London: and the Black Death, 15, 23;
sewage disposal, 27–8, 31–2, 88, 98–
100, 148–9; town ditch, 28;
slaughtering and butchering by-
products, 28–9; soap-makers, 43;
streets, 66–7; mud and mud-throwing, 67; coal-burning, 74–6, 103;
outbreak of plague (1625), 82;
Great Plague (1665), 84–8, 95; Great
Fire (1666), 92–4, 98; rebuilding
after Fire, 96–7; laystalls, 97–9;
waste disposal, 88, 98–9, 101; smoke
and fogs, 102–3, 149, 164; street
lighting, 102; water supply, 104–6,
137–9; nineteenth-century housing
conditions, 131–2, 134–5; cholera,
140, 146, 148; the 'Great Stink'
(1858), 148, see also Thames, river
London 'ague', 104
London Bridge, 64: public garderobes,
31–2; waterworks, 105, 106
London Labour and the London Poor
(Mayhew), 127, 151
London Magazine, 113
Londonderry, Marquis of, 143
Lucas, Dr., 106
Luther, Martin, 20

Macarthur, Sir William, 20 n.
Magna Carta, and removal of weirs, 63
Malthus, T. R., 142
Man and the Flea (Gay), 80
Man and the Mode, The (Etherege), 90
Manchester: pollution of water supply,
139, 160–1; cholera, 146; Irish
population, 153; atmospheric pollu-
tion, 165
Manufacturing Population of England, The
(Gaskell), 152
Marchant's waterworks, 106
Marguerite of Flanders, 40
Marx, Karl, 153
Matilda, Queen, and lepers, 12

Mayhew, Henry, 127: on London
sewers, 148–9, 151
Mead, Dr. Richard, on plague, 91–2
Melcombe (Weymouth) and the Black
Death, 17–18
Mersey, river, 160
Metamorphosis of Ajax, The (Harington),
50–2
Micklem, Nathaniel, 6
Minsheu, John 49
Misson, Henri, on coal-burning, 74–6
Monasteries: lack of cleanliness, 14;
privies, 14
Montaigne, 45
More, Sir Thomas, 48
Moufet, Thomas, 55
Mud and mud-throwing in London, 67
Mus norvegicus (brown rat), 94
Mus rattus (black rat), 94
Musk, 44, 45

Nashe, Thomas, 54, 58–60: on sweating
sickness, 56–7
Naworth Castle accounts, 76
New Bath Guide (Anstey), 108
New London Dispensatory (Salmon), 129
New River, 105, 106
Newcastle: cholera, 146; atmospheric
pollution, 165
Newman, Edward, 137
Nitrous fumes, 165
Nits, 54
Norwich, 59, 95: and the Black Death,
15, 23

Obermeier, 57
Observations ... upon the Burning of
London, 1666 (Rege Sincera), 93
Observer, The, 160
Oliver Twist (Dickens), 138
Ordinance of Labourers (1349), 26
Ornithodoros moubata (form of tick), 57
Orwell, George, 128
Osborne, Francis, 71, 74
Oxford, Charles II's court at, 90

Packard, Vance, 2
Padded clothes and furniture, 49–50
Papon, J. P., 16 n.
Paracelsus (Theophrastus Bombast von
Hohenheim), 22–3, 147
Paris, dirt in streets, 67
Parish Register, The (Crabbe), 102

Pasteurella pestis (plague germ), 19
Paston, Margaret, and Paston Letters, 47, 48
Peasants' Revolt (1381), 37
Pediculus capitis (head louse), 54
Pediculus corporis (body louse), 54
Peele, George, 60
Pembroke, Earl of, 67
Pepys, Elizabeth, 89–90, 100
Pepys, Samuel, 89, 91: on the Great Plague (1665), 84–5; and sewage disposal, 88; notions of hygiene and washing, 89–90; on the Fire of London, 92–3; at Bath, 107–8
Perfumes, 44–6: added to soap, 44; civet, 44–6; on gloves and handkerchiefs, 45
Petrarch, on the Black Death, 15
Philpot, John, 28
Phthirus pubis (crab louse), 55
Place, Francis, 103
Plague, *see* Bubonic plague
Plantus, 45
Pleasant and Delightful Dialogues (Minsheu), 49
Poe, Edgar Allan, 26, 112, 141
Polishers, 76–7
Pompeii, 8–9
Pope, Alexander, 112, 114: on Fleet Ditch, 99
Privies, 50, 88–9
Psychopathia Sexualis (Krafft-Ebing), 4–5
Public Health Act (1875), 155
Pudding Lane, London, 28–9

Quarantine, 18, 92
Queen's Wells, The (Rowzer), 107

Rakers, *see* Scavengers
Raleigh, Sir Walter, 52, 71–2
Ralph of Shrewsbury, Bishop of Bath and Wells, 24
Rathbone Place spring, 106
Rathbone, William, 138
Rats and the plague, 19, 88, 94, 95
Rawson, Marmeduke, 91
Reckitt and Colman survey on public attitudes to cleanliness, 166–7
Relapsing fever, 57–8
Report on the Sanitary Condition of the Labouring Population, The, Chadwick Report (1842), 154–5

Respiratory troubles, 150–1
Rhine, river, industrial pollution of, 162
Rich, Sir Henry (Earl of Holland), 71
Richard I, and regulations for river Thames, 62–3
Richard II, 28, 37
Richard the Raker, 27, 102
Richmond Palace, Harington's water-closet at, 52, 53
Ritual defilement, 2
Robert of Avesbury, on the Black Death, 23–4
Roman baths, 7–10: aqueducts, 7–8; steaming and massage, 8; procedure, 8; in Britain, 9–10
Roman vitriol, 77, 78, 108
Rotherham, atmospheric pollution in, 164
Rotterdam drinking water, 162
Rowzer, Lodowick, 107
Rubbish dumps in London, 98
Rushes for floors, 48–9
Russell, J. C., 23
Russell, Dr. Richard, 107
Russia, cholera in, 141–2, 144, 145

St. Albans, monastic privy, 14
St. Anthony's Fire, 26–7
St. Giles district, London, 132
St. Nicholas shambles, Seacoal Lane, 28
St. Paul's Cathedral, 102–3
Saliva and spitting, 3–4
Salmon-fishing in Thames, 60
Sartre, 6: on sliminess, 1–3
Scavengers, 27
Scottish towns, condition in nineteenth century, 132–4
Sea-bathing, 107
Secretions, 3–4
Semiriechinsk, starting-place of Black Death, 17
Sentimental Journey, A (Sterne), 104
Severn, Miss, 128
Severn, river, 64, 160
Sewage disposal, 27–8, 31–2, 88, 98–100, 139–40, 148–9, 151–2, 157
Shaftesbury, and the Black Death, 24
Shakespeare, 45, 48, 56, 58, 60: quoted, 46, 47
Shambles, 28
Sheffield, grinders' asthma, 150–1
Shelley, quoted, 155

Shoemaker's Holiday, The (Dekker), 30, 45
Short Discourse concerning Pestilential Contagion. . . . (Mead), 91
Sidney, Sir Philip, 60
Silchester, Roman pump, 10
Silver polishes, 77
Skelton, John, 29–30
Slaughter-houses, 28
Sliminess, nature of, 2–3
Smallpox, 104, 112
Smith, James, on Bradford water supply, 139–40
Smoke, 102–3, 149–50, 164: and fogs, 149, 164
Smollett, Tobias, 108
Snow, Dr. John, discovery on cholera, 147–8
Snows Rents, Westminster, 137
Soap and soap-makers, 42–4, 76; use of potash, 42, 43; grades of soap, 42–3; glycerine, 43; soda soap, 43–4; addition of perfume, 44; modern use of soap and detergents, 157–9
Songs of Experience (Blake), 102
Southall, John and Mary, bug destroyers, 127
Southampton, and the Black Death, 18
Spas, 107–8
Spenser, Edmund, 66, 160
Spirillum obermeieri (relapsing fever germ), and *Spirilla* germs, 57, 58
Sproat family, cholera victims, 142–3
Stains, removal of, 76
Starching, 76
Statute of Labourers (1351), 26
Sterne, Laurence, 104
Stews (sweating-houses), 36–8: become brothels, 36–7; closure and revival, 37–8
Stow, John, 32, 65–7, 105: on stews, 37; on soap-makers, 43
Strachey, Lytton, 52
Strype, John, 97–8, 105: on obstructions in Thames, 65
Sulphur dioxide, 165
Sunderland, outbreak of cholera (1831), 142–6
Survey of London (Stow), 32, 65, 105
Sweating sickness, 56–8, 91
Swift, Jonathan, 100, 115–18: *Directions to Servants*, 100, 115–16; on the human body and its functions, 115;

and the Yahoos, 116–17
Szerelmey, Ltd., 103

Table manners, 41–2
Tame, river, pollution of, 161
Taylor, M. R., 25
Tees, river, industrial pollution of, 160
Thackeray, William Makepeace, 117, 118
Thames, river, 29, 32, 60–6, 138, 139, 160: salmon-fishing, 60; care vested in Mayor and corporation (1179), 62; obstruction by weirs, locks, etc., 63–5; rubbish cast into it, 64; London Bridge, 31–2, 64, 105, 106; frosts, 64; source of water supply, 105–6, 157; pollution, 110, 139, 148; the 'Great Stink' (1858), 148
Thermae (Roman baths), 7
Thomas à Becket, St., vermin on his body, 19–20
Thrale, Mrs., 107
Ticks, 57–8
Tiffin and Son, Bug-Destroyers to Her Majesty, 127–8
Timber-framed houses, 94
Times, The, 135
Tower of London, 28, 60, 62
Traditionall Memoyres (Osborn), 71
Travellers and infection, 165–6
Trevelyan, G. M., 101
Tull, Jethro, 120
Tunbridge water, 107
Turkish baths, 8, 34–6
Two Years Ago (Kingsley), 148
Tyler, Wat, 37
Tyne, river, and industrial pollution, 160
Typhoid, 104, 110
Typhus, 55–8, 104

Ulysses (Joyce), 4
Unfortunate Traveller, The (Nashe), 54
Unilever, 157
Uriconium (Wroxeter), bath-buildings, 9
U.S.A.: foam pollution, 159–60; wood-pulp pollution, 161; carbon monoxide, 165

Vienna, and the plague, 18, 84
Villiers, George, Duke of Buckingham, 67, 72. 74

Vincent, Rev. Thomas, 93
Vitruvius, 10

Wales, cholera in, 146
Wallis, John, 77
Walworth, Sir William, 37
Wandle, river, and foam pollution, 160
Ward, Ned, 108
Washing, 104, 136–7: at table, 40–2; cleansing and laundering, 76–7; removal of stains, 76; in mining community, 136–7; wash-houses, 138
Waste disposal, 88, 98–9, 101, *see also* Sewage disposal
Water-closets, 105, 109–11: Harington's invention, 50–3
Water supply, 104–6, 156–7: private waterworks, 105–6; inadequacy, 135–8; water-carriers, 137; pollution, 138–40, 159–63
Waterman, Sir George, 87

Water-pipes, Roman, 10
Weirs on Thames, 63
Weldon, Sir Anthony, on James I, 69–72
Wesley, John, 115
Whitechapel High Street, 66–7
Wilkinson, Kitty, 138
William IV, 144
Windsor: King's stews, 36; baths installed in Castle, 53
Woburn, water-closets at, 109
Wolsey, Cardinal, 48
Wood, Anthony à, 90
Word, J. Riddall, 139
Wood-pulp and water pollution, 161
Wren, Sir Christopher, 94, 96, 102
Wright, Lawrence, 38

Xenopsylla cheopis (plague flea), 19

Yahoos, the, 116–17
York, 91, 95: water supply, 105

CPSIA information can be obtained
at www.ICGtesting.com
Printed in the USA
BVHW051526140422
634164BV00003B/501